Contents

Abbreviations of County Names

Bd	Bedfordshire	Mx	Middlesex
Bk	Buckinghamshire		
Brk	Berkshire	Nb	Northumberland
		Nf	Norfolk
C	Cambridgeshire	Nt	Nottinghamshire
Ch	Cheshire	Nth	Northamptonshire
Co	Cornwall		
Cu	Cumberland	O	Oxfordshire
D	Devonshire	Ru	Rutland
Db	Derbyshire		
Do	Dorset	Sa	Shropshire
Du	Durham	Sf	Suffolk
		So	Somerset
Ess	Essex	Sr	Surrey
		St	Staffordshire
Gl	Gloucestershire	Sx	Sussex
Ha	Hampshire	W	Wiltshire
He	Herefordshire	Wa	Warwickshire
Hrt	Hertfordshire	We	Westmorland
Hu	Huntingdonshire	Wo	Worcestershire
		Wt	Isle of Wight
K	Kent		
		YE	Yorkshire, East Riding
La	Lancashire	YN	Yorkshire, North Riding
Lei	Leicestershire	YW	Yorkshire, West Riding
Li	Lincolnshire		
Lo	London (the former county)		

6

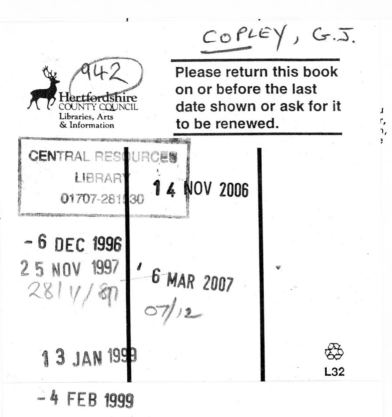

Please renew/return this item by the last date shown.

So that your telephone call is charged at local rate,
please call the numbers as set out below:

	From Area codes 01923 or 0208:	From the rest of Herts:
Renewals:	01923 471373	01438 737373
Enquiries:	01923 471333	01438 737333
Minicom:	01923 471599	01438 737599

L32b

ENGLISH PLACE-NAMES
AND THEIR ORIGINS

ENGLISH PLACE-NAMES AND THEIR ORIGINS

by

G. J. Copley

DAVID & CHARLES: NEWTON ABBOT

ISBN 0 7153 5292 X

First published 1968
Second impression 1971

To L.W.H.P.

Printed in Great Britain
by Redwood Press Limited   Trowbridge   Wilts
for David & Charles (Publishers) Limited
South Devon House   Newton Abbot   Devon

Introduction

Place-names touch upon very many details of the more distant past. Sometimes they provide information that would not otherwise be recoverable, so affording numerous footnotes to history. For instance, our knowledge of the Anglo-Saxon settlement of southern Britain would be much poorer without the information to be had from place-names. There are certain types characteristic of that period which, when plotted on a map, provide an invaluable supplement to the meagre facts and many uncertainties of documentary history and of archaeology. The Scandinavian invaders of four centuries later have also left their characteristic marks on the place-name map: the Danes in the Midlands and North and the Norwegian Vikings in the North-West. Even the well-documented Norman Conquest gains in minor detail from a study of Anglo-Norman names; and the barons who displaced the Saxon thanes from their estates are remembered still in many a village name, such as Stoke Mandeville Bk, though it is seldom that the family who thus gave their name to a village was in possession of that same manor immediately after 1066. These double names mostly begin to appear in the records of the thirteenth century.

All ranks of society, their occupations, their social and other activities, their lives and their deaths are commemorated, as well as the highly complex organisation of Saxon and later medieval society. Even their ironic humour sometimes survives in field-names.

And the face of the land they tended, in all its convolutions of hill and river, valley and pool, its trees, plants, animals and even its insects find mention here and there. The uses of the land, its exploitation by king, noble, abbot and peasant, and the edging forward of the arable into the confines of the forests, are alluded to in shire after shire. And from the accumulation of many scattered details, a broad picture of the constantly changing medieval landscape emerges from the long-forgotten past. Even the very names of numerous Saxon and later men and women survive in the names of the localities where they laboured to win their bread from the soil.

The language ordinary men spoke, evolving slowly century by century and varying in detail from one region to another, is recorded in the names they gave to the places where they settled; and the spellings that occur in the records of successive generations mirror the changes of pronunciation that were taking place without anyone being aware of them. Words that came readily to the lips of the first English settlers, but which have been lost for more than a thousand years from human memory, survive in their descriptions of the countryside around them that we now know as place-names.

Moreover, place-names have a very personal interest for many of us. More than half the surnames we bear are, in origin, the names of places where our ancestors lived; and there are other surnames which were given to our forebears because of the occupations they followed. Some of these, too, enter into place-names and, where a choice of examples was possible in the following pages, place-names that are also surnames have been used.

The total number of English place-names is enormous. There must be more than twelve thousand parishes in England and in each of them there may be several dozen minor names. If we add to these the various kinds of names in the towns and the names of rivers and brooks that belong to no one parish, the number becomes embarrassingly large. The examples chosen are, therefore, those of special interest or ones that are widely known.

CHAPTER 1

People and Places

The complexities of Anglo-Saxon society are mirrored to some extent in the place-names which first came into use before the Norman Conquest or soon after. Every rank and many occupations, humble and lordly, find mention in them. The king's manors are usually named from his title, as in the many Kingstons; and his other landed possessions, such as the Kingswoods Gl, Sr, Wa and Kingsleys Ch, Ha, St were also prefixed by his title. His consort, however, had fewer estates and she is less often commemorated, but the meaning 'queen's manor' is probably the right translation of Quinton Gl, Nth, Wo, which is a compound of *cwēn* and *tūn*.

Of humbler rank was a *wīf*, 'woman' or 'wife', in the place-names Westow (with *stow*, 'a place'), Winestead (with *stede*, 'a place') and Wyton (*tūn*) of the East Riding of Yorkshire. Her newly-married status as a bride (*brȳd*) is indicated in such places as Brid(e)well D, W, or Britford W. The *wella*, 'spring or stream', in these localities was probably thought to have had water of some special quality in promoting fertility; the ford may have been one so shallow that it was easy to cross and so suitable for a bride. The unmarried woman (*mægden*) or maiden is alluded to in numerous places, though the meanings of their names are often doubtful, too. Fertility springs may be referred to in Maidenwell Co, L and in Maidwell Nf; and the original landing-place (*hȳð*) of Maidenhead Brk perhaps gave access from the Thames to an estate owned by a convent. Its members could be called 'maidens' in Middle English.

9

There were several Old English words for a 'warrior' which once, no doubt, were not completely synonymous. Some of these words were also used as personal names with little thought for their original meaning. For instance, *beorn*, 'a hero, a warrior', is indistinguishable in early forms of place-names from the personal name *Beorn(a)* and either may occur in Barnham Sf, Sx and Barnwell C. The word *cempa* presents a similar difficulty in the compound Kempshot Ha, which meant 'the warrior's or *Cempa's* corner of land (*scēat*)'. The modern surname Kemp(e) originated in this Old English name. A somewhat different problem is presented by *secg*, which could mean 'warrior' or 'sedge' or could be used as the by-name *Secg*. In Sedgemoor So (*mōr*) we obviously have the plant-name, but in Sedgeley St (*lēah*) a person is almost certainly referred to. Early forms of the name such as *Secgesleage* and *Seggeslegh* have a genitive singular as the first two syllables, giving the meaning '*Secg's* or the warrior's wood'. Without the -*es*- it would have been more reasonable to render it as 'sedgewood'.

The word *hægstald* and its variant *hagustald* originally described 'the occupant of an enclosure,' a minor man of property. It came to mean 'warrior', though the older meaning is likely in Hexham Nb and in Hestercombe So.

A fragment of forgotten local history is enshrined in the Norfolk place-names Whissonsett and Witchingham. Both localities were readily accessible to invaders moving up the river Wensum, 'the winding one', from the North Sea. The first meant 'the camp or dwelling (*ge-set*) of the pirates (*wīcingas*)' and the second, 'homestead (*hām*) of the pirates'. The first may have been a temporary foothold, the second a permanent settlement of the marauders who harried the east coast long before the beginning of the main Viking invasions. They had sacked Lindisfarne and had raided into Dorset in AD 793, and Jarrow had suffered in the following year. They ceased their raiding for about a generation before returning in greater strength and in 841 East Anglia was attacked. The *Old English Chronicle* states that 'In this year ealdorman *Hereberht* was

10

slain by the heathen and many with him among the people of the Marsh (of Lincolnshire); and the same year, again in Lindsey and in East Anglia and in Kent, many men were slain by the host.' It was perhaps at this time that the *Wīcingas* established themselves beside the river Wensum.

But it was the later, main body of Vikings who so greatly changed the place-nomenclature of northern and eastern England and they are probably commemorated in names such as Wigginton YN and Wigston Lei, Wickenby L and Wiganthorpe YN. All of these have a second element meaning 'farm' or 'village' (ON *bȳ*, *þorp* and OE *tūn*) and a first element *Víkingr*. This may, however, be the Old Norse personal name rather than the noun 'pirate', but it comes to the same thing anyway. Very many of the words noted in this and following chapters are of Old Norse origin, brought in by the Vikings of Denmark or Norway. Their marauding activities, which had begun in the eighth century, extended down the western coasts of Europe and to the whole length of the Mediterranean from the Pillars of Hercules to the coasts of Asia Minor. The raiding and settlement in England was but part of a far larger process of Scandinavian expansion.

The leaders of these armies are rarely commemorated in English place-names, though the *jarl* who once owned the shieling (*sǽtr*) of Yarlside La was more likely to have been a Norwegian than a Dane, for the counties of Cumberland, Westmorland and Lancashire were settled largely by men from western Scandinavia who had sojourned for a while in the Shetlands, the Orkneys, then the Western Isles and the north of Ireland. A contemporary Anglo-Saxon nobleman might be an *eorl*, which has become 'earl' in modern English and is cognate with Old Norse *jarl*. As there was an OE personal name *Eorl*, and as 'Earl' came to be used as a title after the Norman Conquest, it is difficult to know which of these meanings should be assumed in place-names such as Arleston Db or Earlshaw Nt, which are compounds with *tūn*, 'farm' and *sceaga*, 'wood'. On the other hand, medieval records show that Earl's Barton Nth was held

11

by a twelfth-century Earl of Huntingdon and that Earl's Croome Wo belonged to the Earls of Warwick. (For the meaning of Croome, see p 59.)

A Scandinavian of lower, though still prosperous, rank was a *hǫldr*, as in Holderness YE, which is best rendered as 'peninsula (ON *nes*) of the yeoman'. Still further down the social scale was the freedman (ON *leysingi*). Lazenby YN and Lazonby Cu contain either this word or a personal name identical with it in spelling. At the servant level, we have ON *drengr*, which, too, was used as a by-name. Dringhouses YW and Drinsey L, Nt have this word, the first obvious in meaning, but the second having the original termination *hagi*, an Old Norse word for a grazing enclosure.

Old English words for the humbler orders are more numerous. The variant forms *cnafa* (our word 'knave', which has changed in meaning) or *cnapa*, both connoting 'boy or servant' and both cognate with German 'knabe', 'boy', as well as the personal name *Cnapa* and its Old Norse equivalent *Knapi*, give Knavenhill Wo and Knapton Nf, YE, YW. Which of these variants enters into these place-names is uncertain. OE *boi(a)*, with the same meanings, is rarely recorded before the fourteenth century and was also a personal name. One or other of them is found in the frequently recurring Boyton, in Boycott Bk, Sa, Wo and in Boythorpe Db, YE. The Middle English *grome*, 'groom, boy or servant', lies behind the first syllable of Groombridge K, Sx.

Occupation names of the Anglo-Saxon period are not uncommon in our place-names. The word *bæcestre*, 'baker', and origin of the surname Baxter, is the first part of the place-name Baxterley Wa; and the shoemaker, *sūtere* in Old English, *sútari* in Old Norse, gave his name to Sutterton and Sutherby in Lincolnshire. The chapman (OE *cēapmann*) or merchant, besides being ancestral to the surname Chapman, had some obscure connection with a valley (*slæd*) at Chapmanslade W; and his North Country counterpart, ON *kaupmaðr*, had a nook of land (*vrá*) at Capernwray La and another was presumably chief man in the hamlet of Copmanthorpe YW. Metal workers seem to have been ubiquitous since the Bronze Age, hence the numerous Smiths of today and place-names such as Smethwick Ch, St, Smeaton Co, YN, YW and Smethcote or -cott Ha, St. Some of the early dwellers at the Smeatons acquired this as a surname when they migrated elsewhere.

In the wide forests of early England there was employment for many woodmen and their humble dwellings (*cot*) existed at many a Woodmancote or -cott. Another woodland worker, important until quite recent times, was the charcoal-burner (OE *colestre*); Colsterdale YN and Colsterworth L were once the scenes of his activities. The forester (Old French *forestier*) had charge of the local woodland occupations at Frosterley Du, the final syllable of which is *lēah*, probably with its older meaning of 'wood' rather than 'clearing'; and in Cockfosters Hrt we have an enigmatic place-name which may have meant 'head forester'. One of his main duties would have been to regulate the activities of huntsmen (OE *hunta*), whose work is referred to in numerous place-names including Huntingford Do, Gl, Huntington He, Sa and Huntley Gl. In the last of these instances a personal name *Hunta* may occur, as it probably does also in the shire and town name Huntingdon (*dūn*); but the other names just quoted have early spellings showing the genitive plural and they can therefore only refer to 'hunts*men*', A presumed Old English word *huntere* is probably found in Hunston Sf and Hunterly Du. The meaning of the latter name would have been 'the hunter's barrow' (*hlāw*).

To the peasantry, the bailiff (*ge-rēfa*) was an important and unpopular local official, of whom Chaucer said that they were afraid of him '*as of the deeth*'. Reaveley Nb, Rayton Nt and Reepham L preserve a distant memory of him and suggest that his office may sometimes have been a very profitable one, enabling him to acquire an estate or a piece of woodland. The sheriff (*scīr-(ge)-rēfa*) was on a far higher social plane as the king's chief executive officer for the shire and it is less surprising that he should have possession of a manor. In the name Cherry Orchard Wo, we have an example of a substitution of a new word for an original one when the older had changed out of recognition, for

13

'cherry' has been substituted for 'sheriff' in modern English. In the Kentish Shears Green there has been a similar change, with a more familiar word replacing the less familiar. Shrewton W and Shroton Do reveal how far the old English word for 'sheriff' could change without substitution. They were both 'sheriffs' manors'.

Before the importation of cane sugar, honey was used for sweetening and, fermented, was made into mead. The beekeeper (*bīcere*), therefore, had a very important function in the community, sometimes having a specialised establishment, a 'bee-farm', for the production of honey. Bickerton Ch, D, He, Nb, were such farms (*tūn*) or, perhaps, simply enclosures to protect the hives; and the Lancashire place-names Bickerstaffe and Bickershaw were originally the 'bee-keeper's landing-place' (*stæð*) and 'wood' (*sceaga*).

Professional entertainers, minstrels, tumblers and mummers were joyous relief to a peasantry who lived precariously from harvest to harvest and who, in a bad year, died in great numbers from starvation or its attendant diseases. An occasional visit to the village by a minstrel (*hearpere*) was an event to be enjoyed to the full and remembered for long afterwards. Payment could not be in money but would have been made in kind, mainly food and drink. It is not easy to imagine why the harper should give his name to any natural feature, but in Harperwell YW he and a spring are associated; in Harperley Du the association is with a wood. There is the possibility that a confusion has occurred in the latter name between *hearpere* and *hearpene*, 'a nightingale', though County Durham is beyond the limits of the bird's normal penetration from the south, at least in modern times.

And no less strange is the occurrence of *bēmere*, 'a trumpeter', in the place-names Bemerton W and Bemersley St, though if the word were used as a nickname, it could well have been caught up in the naming of a place. It would not then have been a true occupation name.

In Chapter 6 some of the occupation names to be found in the towns are considered.

14

CHAPTER 2

Animal, Bird and Insect Names

Just as titles such as *secg* and *eorl* could be used as personal names, so could those of animals. Presumably a man called *Wulf* was thought to have some of the characteristics of a wolf. It is recounted in the early eighth-century poem 'Beowulf', that warriors of the Gēat tribe named *Eofor* (boar) and *Wulf* were richly rewarded by their king for slaying the aged *Ongenþēow*, king of the Swedes; and another Old English poem, the fragment '*Wulf* and *Eadwacer*', is a woman's lament for her exiled lover, *Wulf*. There is no hint of disapprobation in the poems for these names and the animal names applied to human beings are accepted as ordinary practice. Another poem, '*Dēor*', is the lament of a minstrel of that name, which could mean 'animal or deer'. *Hengist* and *Horsa* are probably known to most schoolboys as the leaders of the conquest of Kent in the middle of the fifth century. The *Anglo-Saxon Chronicle* records their exploits in the annals from 449 to 473. Their names meant 'stallion' and 'horse'.

These people belong to the period just before and during the Anglo-Saxon conquest of England, but animal names continued to be given to people for several centuries afterwards, even including those which, to modern ways of thinking, are derogatory. The kite, a hawk that was still widely spread in nineteenth-century Britain but is now almost extinct here, is a scavenger and carrion-eater. Its Old English name was *putta* or *puttoc* and the latter name appears among the signatures to a West Saxon charter of AD 739 and was obviously therefore borne by a man of substance. There was a late seventh-century bishop of

15

Rochester called *Putta*; and the endorsement of a Mercian charter of 801 is signed by a certain *Wigga*, which meant 'beetle' (as in 'earwig'). Later Mercian charters are signed by this man, or another of the same name, with the addition of the title *ealdormann*, which was applied to the chief officers of the shire and to the highest rank of noblemen. Of rather a different kind was the signature *Bola*, 'tree-trunk, bole', to a charter of the same period.

It is difficult to believe that these names were used without any thought of their basic meanings, yet it is likely that contemporary attitudes to animals were unlike our own. However, what has to be borne in mind is that place-names containing words for animals, birds, fishes and insects may, in fact, have referred to men, or rarely, to women.

Place-names having a habitative word for their ending, such as *-hām*, 'homestead', *-tūn*, 'farm', or *-cot*, 'cottage', will usually have had a personal name for the first element. That this is not always so is exemplified by a name such as Foxcot(e), Foxcott or Foscot(t), which is one form or another occurs all over England. It would be strange if so many men named Fox were to have been inhabitants of cottages; but foxes and their earths occurred almost everywhere and there is little doubt that this place-name meant 'fox-earth'. Foxley He, Nf, Nth, W was a wood frequented by foxes and Foxton C, Leî, Nb, YN is said to mean 'farm infested with foxes', though it is hard to see why there was not a personal name *Fox* that would explain some at least of these farm-names.

Domestic animals were often significant enough to characterise places and give names to them. For example, Bulmer Ess YN, has genitive plural forms which show that it meant 'bulls' (*bula*), lake (*mere*)', whereas Bullingdon O, with a genitive singular, may have been 'bull's hill (*dūn*)' or '*Bula*'s hill'. Bulwick Nth was a farm where, presumably, bulls were fattened and Bulcamp Sf an enclosed field (*camp*) where they were pastured. In Bowness We, we have the Old Norse *boli*, 'a bull', combined with ON *nes*, 'a headland'. The modern term 'stirk', meaning 'a bullock, a

16

heifer', has its origin in OE *stīrc* or *stȳr(i)c* and is found in the names Stirchley Sa, Stretton Ch and Strickland We. The related word *stēor* (our 'steer'), lies behind the first syllable of Stourbridge C, site of the greatest of the annual trade fairs of medieval England. The name of the town Stourbridge Wo means, however, 'bridge over the river Stour'.

The more general term 'calf', which had the same spelling in Old English, occurs in many place-names. ON *kalfr* cannot be distinguished from it in such northern names as Calton Db, St or Cawton YN, which were farms (*tūn*) specialising in calf-rearing. Calverton Bk, Nt and Calverley YW have the genitive plural *calfra*; the West Saxon form *cealf*, in which 'c' became palatalised to 'ch', is the explanation for Chaldon Do, Sr with *dūn*, 'a hill' and for Chalton Bd and Chawton Ha, both with *tūn*. Bullocks (*bulluc*) were reared in a clearing (*lēah*) at Bulkeley Ch and in an enclosure (*worþig*) at Bulkworthy D.

But cows (OE *cū*) were probably the commonest domestic animals then as now, for they were valuable in providing meat, milk and offspring. Names such as Cowhill Gl and Cowden K (with *denn*; 'woodland pasture') are to be found in most counties. Of the many Cowleys, the Gloucestershire and Lancashire ones meant 'clearing for cows', but others (Bk, D, Mx, O) have personal names, *Cufa* or *Cofa* as first elements. The very frequent minor name Cowleaze, applied to fields or farms, have *lǣs* as final element and meant 'cow pasture'. In Keele St we have the plural *cȳ* (compare Scottish 'kine') combined with *hyll* and in Kyloe Nb, with *lēah*.

The ox (*oxa*) was the normal draught animal for ploughing and hauling until quite recent times and it is of fairly common occurrence in place-names. Besides Oxford, there are at least three Oxtons Ch, Nt, YW and Oxley St as well as the widely distributed Oxleaze as a minor name. And *hrīðer* or its variant *hrȳðer* was used in Old English as a word for 'ox' as well as meaning 'cattle' in general. It gives rise to Rotherfield Ha, O, Sx, 'open country (*feld*) where oxen or cattle were kept' and Rotherhithe Lo was a 'landing-place (*hȳð*) for cattle'. There was also the word *weorf*, used of a draught animal or beast of burden, from which the first element of names such as Warley Sa, Wo and Worley Wo are derived. As so often in these and following compounds with words for grazing animals, the second element means 'clearing', a place where grass could be eaten, though it has to be remembered that grazing animals were also turned out into woodland to find their keep; and not only when grass was in poor supply.

It is unlikely that peasants kept horses during the Anglo-Saxon period, unless they had prospered greatly. They were used mainly for riding and seldom for draught work, though the lower border of the Bayeux Tapestry, at the point where Duke William's messengers came to Guy, Count of Ponthieu, depicts a heavy horse pulling a plough. Artist's licence, perhaps. However, the Old English word *hors* is the first element of Horsham Nf, Sx, Horstead K, Nf, Sx and the common name Horsley. In Hursley Ha, W we have the related word *hyrse*, 'a mare'. The stallion (*hengest*) enters into the name Henstridge So, compounded with *hrycg*, 'a ridge', into Hinksey Brk, with *ēg* 'island or water-meadow', and Hinxworth Hrt, 'an enclosure (*worð*) for stallions'. A herd of horses, a stud (OE *stōd*), is indicated by Studley O, W, Wa, YW and Studland Do. Prehistoric, Roman or Saxon enclosures of various kinds were used as corrals and were called 'studfolds' (*stōd-fald*). Stutfall (Castle) K was originally a Roman fort; and there are Stotfolds in Bedfordshire and County Durham. A number of field-names (Gl, Nt, Nth, Wa, YE, YN), none of which now corresponds with surviving enclosures, probably were once merely fenced fields for horses.

The Old English *fola*, 'foal', and Old Norse *foli* are difficult to distinguish in some place-names, though the Devonshire Fulla-moor must be from the Old English word. The West Riding name Follifoot refers to the Norse sport of horse-fighting; the -foot syllable being derived from OE *feoht*; and the names Hesket(h) Cu, La, YN preserve a memory of Viking horse-racing, being compounds of ON *hestr*, 'horse, stallion' (cognate with OE *hengest*) and ON *skeið*, 'a race-course'. But the generic name

18

for 'horse' in the Danelaw was *hross*, which is preserved in Rosthwaite La in combination with ON *þveit*, 'a clearing' or, in this name, 'a paddock'. It could be that there was a metathesised form of OE *hors*, namely *hros*, and that it entered into such a name as Rosewain Cu, the second element of which is derived from OE (*ge*)-*winn*, 'a fight', in which case we should have a further reference to horse-fighting. Rossall La was probably OE *hros-halh*, meaning 'corner of land where horses were kept'.

In this same north-western region of England yet another term for horse was in use, namely ON *kapall*. This word is ultimately from Latin *caballus*, 'a nag', but immediately from Old Irish *capall*. It is, of course, cognate with French *cheval* and English 'cavalry'. *Kapall* is one of several additions to the Viking vocabulary picked up during the sojourn in Ireland. It underlies the first word in Capel Craig Cu and Capplerigg We, the latter with ON *hryggr*, 'a ridge'. Other instances of these borrowings from Old Irish are *cros*, 'a cross' and *erg*, 'a shieling, or a hill pasture'. (See pp 91 and 115).

Wool and cloth were the main exports of Anglo-Saxon England and continued for centuries to hold that primacy. Sheep, therefore, were a highly important element in the economy and in the lives of ordinary men and women. Many a place took its name from these animals. The generic word for them was *scēp* in the Anglian, Kentish and West Saxon dialects; *scīp* in Old Northumbrian; and *scēap* or *scīep* in earlier West Saxon. These variations in the word largely explain the modern variations in place-names: Shep- and Sheep- from West Saxon *scēap*; but Shap- and Shop- occur where the stress shifted from the first part of the diphthong (*éa*) to the second part (*eá*). The modern forms in Ship- come from West Saxon *scīep* or from its later development *scȳp*. In the north, Ship- and Skip- are from the Northumbrian, with the Sk- due to Old Norse influence. In a few instances the modern place-names begin with S- (eg Sapcote, Lei) as a result of Anglo-Norman influence on the pronunciation and spelling.

In every region there were sheep farms: Shepton So, Shipton

Bk, Do, Gl, Ha, O, Sa, Sx, YW, Skipton YN, YW; and many woodland clearings were given over to their pasturage: Shipley Db, Du, Nb, Sa, Sx, YW, Shepley YW; Shapwick Do, So, Shopwyke Sx and very many more with other terminations. In Rampton C, Nt we have OE *ramm* combined with *tūn* and in Ramsbottom La with *botm*, 'valley floor'. Wetheral Cu with *halh* and Wetherley C with *lēah* also refer to rams (OE *weðer*); and *hnocc* in Nocton L and Notton YW has a similar meaning. Young animals are particularised in Lambley Nb, Nt, Lambton Du and Lambeth Lo. The last instance is a reference to a landing-place (*hȳð*) beside the Thames from which lambs could be taken for fattening on the Lambeth Marsh, which survives as a street-name.

The sty (*stigu*) was probably not in common use as a pen for pigs, though Housty and Houxty Nb both mean 'hog sty'. The servant responsible for it was called a *stīg-weard*, 'sty-guardian', which gives the modern names Steward and Stewart (cf Thornton Steward YN, which *c* AD 1100 was in the possession of the steward to the Earl of Richmond. By then, however, stewards were senior household officials). But most pigs were left free to range on hills and in woods, with some herds confined to specialised farms. Swinton La, YN, YW illustrate the latter point and Swindon Gl, St, W, 'swine (*swīn*)-hill (*dūn*)', the former. The ability of pigs to thrive in places too wet for most other domestic animals may explain place-names such as Swinburn Nb and Somborne Ha, both compounds of *swīn* and *burna*, 'brook'. Swinbrook O, with OE *brōc* has the same meaning. The four Swinfords Brk, K, St, Wo similarly imply pig-farming close to streams. The ON word *gríss*, surviving as the dialect word 'grice', is found in the Westmorland name Grisdale, which is broadly similar in meaning to Swinden YW, the latter from OE *denu*, 'a valley', the former from ON *dalr*, 'a valley, a dale'. Gristhwaite YN was a 'clearing (*þveit*) for (young) pigs'.

Goats (OE *gāt*, ON *geit*) were probably commoner than today, perhaps because of their ability to survive with little or no human help, for they seem to be able to digest almost any kind

20

of plant-food, even the coarsest. Their hair and hides, kid-meat, milk and cheese had a certain economic value, too. Together with those of sheep, cattle and pigs, their bones have been recovered from Anglo-Saxon dwelling-sites, although those of goats were the least numerous. Gatcomb(e) So, Wt were valleys (*cumb*) in which they were pastured; Gateley Nf is a type of compound familiar by now to the reader; and Gotham Nt was presumably a homestead (*hām*) where goats were kept. Gateshead Du may have been a headland on which they roamed free, but the name may well refer to a heathen custom of setting up an animal's head on a pole. (See pp 128–9.)

The related word OE *gǣten*, 'a kid', is found in the two Hertfordshire names Gaddesden (with *denu*, 'valley'), and Gatesbury (with *burh*, 'fort'), though a personal name with the same spelling is possible in either. The he-goat, *hæfer*, occurs in Hathersage Db combined with *ecg*, 'escarpment' and in Hertford YE. A confusion with OE *hæfera* or ON *hafri*, 'oats', could easily happen and certainty about the derivation of these names is impossible. Another word for 'kid', *ticcen*, is the origin of the first syllable of Tichborne Ha (*burna*) and Ticehurst Sx (*hyrst*, 'a wooded hill').

Dogs had been domesticated as early as the New Stone Age and their bones have been recovered from the cattle enclosures, the 'causewayed camps' characteristic of that period. These dogs were no doubt trained to help in hunting and herding and in giving warning of human or animal predators. The OE word *dogga* is rare in place-names; Dogbury Do, 'dog-hill (*beorg*)' is one of the few early instances; the few dozen others seem to belong to the post-medieval period, like The Isle of Dogs Lo, which has not been noted in records before 1593; in the fourteenth century it was called '*marsh of Stebenhithe*', that is, '*Stybba*'s landing-place (*hȳð*)', the modern Stepney. The alternative *hund* is frequent in earlier usage, as in the street-name Hungate Lincoln, York, Market Weighton. This is similar in meaning to Dog Lane, a Staffordshire hamlet. Hunton Ha may have been a dog-breeding farm or, more probably, it may contain the personal name *Hund*. Puppies or fox-cubs are implied in Whelpley Bk, Sx, W, though the personal name *Hwelp* may be involved. If this is so, it is very strange that men of this name should each be associated with a wood or clearing and that otherwise the name should be very rare and only associated with localities where foxes, rather than men, would be expected.

The whole menagerie of wild animals is represented in our place-names, for most kinds were far commoner then than now and so were more likely to characterise a place and give it a name. The red deer, naturally a denizen of thick forests, and the roe, of a more varied habitat, are the only truly native deer, although it is thought that fallow deer were introduced into Britain in Roman times. The sika, a native of Japan and Manchuria, is a recent import and irrelevant to the present purpose. The OE word *dēor* meant 'animal' as well as 'deer', but in names such as Darley Db, Durley Ha and Deerhurst Gl the association with woodland makes the meaning 'deer' the more likely one; the idea of 'animals' (in general) seems less apt. The male of the species was *bucc*, exemplified probably in Buckton He, Nb, YE and possibly also in Buxton Nf and Buckfast D. In the last two, however, a man *Bucc* is equally likely, possessor of the farm (*tūn*) or of the stronghold (*fæstenn*). More usually the male deer was called *heorot* ('hart'), as in Hartford Gl, Ch, Nb, Hertford Hrt and Hartburn Nb, YE. Harthill Db, YE, YW and Hartley Brk, Ha, K, So are further instances. The ON cognate, *hjǫrtr*, occurs in Harter Fell Cu and Hartwith YW, the latter terminating originally in ON *viðr*, 'a wood', which is itself cognate with OE *wudu*, 'wood'. And the female, *hind*, is exemplified by such names as Hi(e)ndley La, Nb, YW and Hindhead Sr.

Presumably the words for deer already mentioned referred to the red species since there is a distinct word for the roebuck, namely *rā*. The ON equivalent is *rá*, but there was quite a distinct word *rá* meaning 'landmark or boundary' and confusion between them must often have occurred. In names such as Rogate Sr and Roecombe Do, Old Norse elements are highly improbable as these are regions far from Scandinavian settlement; but Rae

Burn Cu may well have been a boundary rather than a brook frequented by roe deer and the headland called Rayhead YW is similarly ambiguous. Reigate Sr involves the OE word *rǣge*, 'the roe hind'.

Place-names involving the fox were considered earlier (p 16), but that other much-hunted creature, the hare, as fascinating in its spring courtship to our ancestors as to us and the object of much superstition, is worthy of brief mention here. Haredene W was a valley (*denu*) where they were commonly seen and Harley Sa, YW was perhaps a clearing (*lēah*) that they frequented. But this name and Harewood Ha, La may contain *hār*, 'hoar, grey with lichen' or its secondary and occasional meaning of 'boundary'. Yet early forms of Harewood He, YW strongly suggest that their first element is indeed *hara*, 'a hare'.

The rabbit was not introduced into England before the twelfth century, but it soon came to be valued as a source of meat and for its fur. By the early twentieth century it was among the three or four commonest mammalian pests, exerting a harmful influence on agriculture by destroying grazing, crops and young trees. The word 'rabbit' is a late Middle English borrowing from French, but this term was less often used than 'cony', which is also a loan-word from French and ultimately from Latin *cuniculus*, which is still the specific name for the animal.

'Cony' itself is rare in place-names (eg Conitor D), but *coninger*, 'a rabbit-warren', is widespread as a minor name in such modern forms as Coneygrey Nt, Coney Geer Nth, Conigree He and so on. Rabbit warrens were once deliberately constructed as raised mounds of earth into which the animals could easily burrow. At Huntingdon Warren on Dartmoor, several such mounds were swarming with rabbits even at the end of the myxomatosis epidemic. Isolation from infected communities had preserved these from the disease. The word 'warren', common among minor place-names, is from Old North French *warenne*, 'a game preserve'. It is in origin a Germanic word, related to OE *weard*, 'watch, ward, guard' and the guardian of a warren was a *warener*, which gives the surname Warner.

23

One of the rabbit's natural enemies, the weasel (or possibly the marten), OE *mearð*, occurs as the first element in Mar(t)ley Sf, Wo, YW. Another enemy is the badger, though foxes, rabbits and badgers have been known to share the same large set; enmity is not, it seems, permanent between them.

The word 'badger' itself is rare in place-names formed before the eighteenth century, but the related word *bagga* is found in the names of most counties. Its woodland habitat is indicated in Bagley Brk, Sa, So, YW and in Bagshaw Db (with *sceaga*, 'a copse'). In the name Bagshot Sr, the second element *scēat*, 'a corner of land', may suggest this animal's preference for haunts remote from man, his only enemy. Another Old English word badger, *grǣg*, is the same as the word for 'grey' and in the latter form was still a synonym for 'badger' until recent times. It is found in the place name Grazeley Brk, which is not a woodland name, as its second element was *sol*, 'a wallowing place'. Gresty Ch is a compound of *grǣg* and *stīg*, 'a path'.

Just as the common noun *bagga* is indistinguishable from the personal name *Bacga* (though the latter certainly occurs in a name like Bagworth Lei, which has a habitative terminal), so *brocc*, in origin a Celtic word, may be confused with the Old English personal names *Brocc* and *Broca*, men who were nicknamed 'badger'. The word *brōc*, 'a brook' is also a cause of confusion. However, woodland names such as Brockhurst Wa and possibly Brockley Nb, So refer to the animal, whereas Brockham Sr with *hām*, 'homestead' and Browston Sf, with *tūn*, 'farm', contain a personal name.

Of the smaller creatures, *frogga* is well represented by such places as Frogmore D, Ha, Hrt, W which has *mere*, 'a pool' as final element and Frogmore Bk, Hrt with *mōr*, 'marshland'. Hertfordshire has, in all, six Frogmores, two of them (in Tring and in Rickmansworth) with *mōr* (and probably the one in Hemel Hempstead too), one in *mere* (St Stephen's parish), an indeterminate one for lack of early forms (in Aston) and one that was originally *Focga*'s *ham* (in Walden). This last one has been influenced in form by the proximity of other Frogmores and it has unconsciously been made to conform to their pattern. The related word *frosc*, *frox*, *forsc*, also meaning 'a frog', occurs in Frostenden Sf (with *denu*) and Froxfield Ha, W (*feld*, 'open country'); and *tāde*, 'a toad', occurs in Tadley Ha, though in Taddiford D, Ha we have the variant *tādige*. *Padde* and *padduc*, with the same meaning, is uncommon, the first form being exemplified in Padbrook K and the second in Padbrook D. Early spellings of the Devonshire name such as *Padokbrok* AD 1291, clearly indicate the derivation of the first element.

BIRDS

Only the more widespread or very distinctive birds were separately named. The finches, so varied to modern eyes, were lumped together as *finca* or *pinca*, both of which are evocative of the chaffinch's call. If others of this group were separately named, they did not enter into the naming of places unless one or other of the few words with lost meanings (eg *gannok*, *nattok*) referred to birds; but this is very unlikely. However, *finca* enters into Finchale Du, 'corner of land (*halh*) frequented by finches'; and perhaps into Fincham Nf, though a personal name is more likely with a habitative terminal such as *hām*. Pinkhurst Sr, Sx contains the variant form and had the meaning 'finch-copse (*hyrst*)'.

The Old English word for the cuckoo, *gēac*, one of the most distinctive of birds, is found in Exbourne D and Yaxley Hu; and its Old Norse cognate, *gaukr*, in Gowthorpe Nf, La, YE, YN and in the five places called Gawthorpe in the West Riding; but here again a personal name is likely for the same reason as before. And the cuckoo's habits seem to have been well known to the Saxons, for one of their riddles that has survived refers to the bird's use of foster-parents and of the fledgling's ejection of other young from the nest.

The lark (*lāwerce*), no doubt a table delicacy then as it is among the barbarous today, is represented in Larkhill C, Ess, W and in Laverstoke, -stock Bk, Ha, W, where *stoc* meant simply 'place'. The Old English for 'swallow', *swealwa*, had a secondary meaning, 'whirlpool' or 'rushing water', which survives in the river-name Swale Brk, K, YN. But Swalcliffe O and Swallowcliffe W are far enough from any 'rushing' stream to make it very probable that the bird is involved. The second element *clif* refers to a steep slope rather than to a cliff in the modern sense. Yet a slope was hardly the birds' nesting-place, but rather a locality where they could sport on the wing in rising air currents as gliders do.

The corvines are distinctive enough to have been separately named and they figure in many place-names. There is the usual difficulty that the names of the birds could be used of persons, as in Roxton Bd, L or Roxby YN which have ON *Hrókr*; but in Rockley W, with OE *hrōc*, or Rookwith YN, made up of ON *hrókr* and ON *viðr*, 'a wood', the rook is obviously a more likely inhabitant. And the same is true of the frequently-recurring Crawley and of Crowhurst Sx, which are compounds of OE *cráwe*, 'a crow', with words for woods. ON *kráka*, 'crow' or 'raven' gives the improbable place-name Crackpott YN, in which the second element, ME *potte*, refers to a deep pit. The modern term 'pot-hole' also contains the Middle English word.

The raven (OE *hræfn*, ON *hrafn*), was an ominous bird and battle-episodes in Old English poetry sometimes mention their clamour as they wheeled above the struggling hosts. In both languages 'Raven' was a common personal name, occurring in place-names such as Ravensthorpe Nth, YN and perhaps Ravenscroft Ch. Ravensden Bd, however, is more likely to have meant 'ravens' valley (*denu*).'

Several sorts of birds of prey were far commoner and more widely distributed than today. The former presence of the kite, (*cýta*) is revealed by names such as Kidbrook(e) Lo, Sx or Kitley D. Another name for it, 'glead' (OE *gleoda*), a word related to the verb 'glide' (a characteristic of its flight), is represented by Gledhill and Gledhow YW, the latter having ON *haugr*, 'hill' as its ending. Yet a third name for the kite, *putta*, has already been alluded to as a personal name (pp 15–16) and among place-names Puttenham and Putney Sr are instances of the bird-name applied to a man and to a place. In Putley He, the bird is almost certainly referred to.

The distribution of place-names that suggest the former presence of eagles (OE *earn*) in England shows that few counties were once without them. Ar(e)ley Ch, La, St, Wa, Wo, Arn(e)-cliff(e) YN, YW, Yarnfield So, St, W, Yes Tor D, Eridge Sx and Arnwood Ha do not include all possible instances. Only East Anglia and the East Midlands seem to have been outside the range of the eagle's habitat, but the publication of place-name studies for Norfolk and Suffolk may yet fill in those blanks on the distribution map. In the names Arnold Nt, YE, which are compounded with *halh*, 'a corner of land', we may have a man's name *Earn(a)* rather than that of the bird.

There seems to have been no differentiation by name of the various kinds of hawk (OE *hafoc*, ON *haukr*). A personal name is likely in Hawksworth YW and possibly in Hauxwell YN, but place-names such as Hawkhill Nb and Haw(k)ridge Bk, Brk, So refer to the bird. The buzzard (OE *wrocc*) soared above Wraxall Do, So, W, Wroxall Wa, Wt (both with *halh*), Wroxham Nf (*hām*) and Wroxton O (*stān*, 'a stone').

Game-birds, including some that we should not find palatable, were of much interest to a peasantry few of whom could enjoy meat frequently and many kinds of them find mention in place-names. Some, like the crane, last bred in the Fens towards the end of the Tudor period; others, like the various kinds of ducks and pigeons, are now with us in greater numbers because the predators that once held their numbers in check are much diminished in their distribution and in their total population.

The word crane (OE *cran*, *cron*, *corn*) is, however, ambiguous, having been applied also to the heron or another related bird. Complications thicken because of the existence of another word for heron, namely *hrāgra*, as in Rawreth Ess, which meant 'heron brook' (OE *rið*). Our word 'heron' does not appear until Middle English, where it is a loan-word from Old High German via Old French. And the various terms for 'crane' are widespread in the shires in names such as Cranbo(u)rne Do, Ha, Cranfield Bd, Cranford Mx, Nth and Cranmore So, the last of which has *mere*, 'a pool', as its ending. These names are all from *cran*. From *corn* or *cron* we get Cor(e)ley Sa, Wa, Cornbrook La, Sa and Cornwood D, Wo. The variant *cranuc* lies behind the first element in Crankshaw La, with *sceaga*, 'copse' and Conksbury Db, which may have meant 'crane's fort', but it is more reasonable to assume a personal name, *Cran(n)uc*, in this compound. The ON *trani*, 'crane', gives Tranmere Ch and Tranmoor YW, with many more besides.

The duck tribe appears in Doughton Gl, Nf, which originally meant 'duck (*dūce*) farm (*tūn*)'; and Duckworth La may have meant much the same, for a *worð*, 'enclosure', was sometimes associated with a homestead and came to have the meaning 'farm', an evolution of meaning similar to that of *tūn*. Another term for 'duck' was OE *ened*, as in Enborne Brk and Endcliff Db, which seems to have meant 'sloping ground (*clif*) frequented by ducks'. And the goose gives name to Goosey Brk, 'goose-island (*ēg*)', Gosford D, O, Wa, Gosforth Cu, Nb (with *ford* also) and Gosport Ha, 'goose market'. The ending -port is from OE *port* meaning 'town, market'. It was derived from either Latin *portus*, 'harbour' or *porta*, 'gateway'. The sense 'harbour' is found in place-names like Portland Do (simply *Port* in early documents) and Portbury So. The Latin *porta* was the origin of OE *port* in Portgate Nb, the name for a gap in the Roman Hadrian's Wall where it is pierced by the Roman Watling Street; here the meaning is 'gateway', so that the Northumberland name is repetitive (tautological).

The swan, which we would find almost uneatable, was a favourite dish at medieval banquets and was no doubt enjoyed in earlier times. Swanbourne Brk and Swanmere Ha have the bird-name, OE *swan*; but Swanton K, Nf, Swanage Do (*wīc*), Swancote Wo and Swanley K more probably contain *swān*, 'herdsman, peasant (swain)' or the personal name *Swān*, as first element. OE *elfitu*, also meaning 'swan', occurs in Elvetham Ha (with *hamm*, 'a water-meadow'), and Eldmire YN (with ON

28

mýrr, 'mire, bog'). Elterwater La has ON *elptr*, a cognate of *elfitu*, and meant 'swan-lake'.

The keeping of pigeons for their eggs and flesh may have begun in the Anglo-Saxon period, but place-names referring to them are seldom recorded before 1600 and only a few surviving dove-cotes are much older. The usual term for dove was OE *culfre*, giving Cullercoats Nb, a compound with *cot* meaning 'dove-cotes'; Culverton Bk has *dūn*, 'hill' and Culverden K has *denn*, 'woodland pasture'. Culverhouse, like Dovehouse, survives here and there as a minor name. The dove (OE *dūfe* and ON *dúfa*) also gave rise to such names as Duffield Db, YE and Dufton We, which may have been a 'farm frequented by doves' or one specialising in their rearing.

Several generic terms for birds are worthy of brief notice. The word 'fowl' (OE *fugol*) did not acquire its meaning of a tame domestic bird until the sixteenth century. The familiar Biblical phrase 'the fowls of the air' has not this restricted sense. Fowlmere C and, of identical derivation, Fulmer Bk refer to waterfowl; Foulmead K, with *mǣd*, 'meadow', and Fulshaw Ch, with *sceaga*, 'copse', imply other kinds. In Fugglestone W and Fulstone YW, originally identical, we have the personal name *Fugol* and *tūn*, 'farm'. In Birdbrook Ess, Birdham Sx (*hām*) and Bridgemere Ch, the first element is OE *bridd*, the origin of our word 'bird'.

OE *hana*, 'a cock', used as a personal name in Hanworth L, Mx, refers to the male bird in Hampole YW (*pōl*, 'pool') and Hanford Ch, Sa, in which places the moorhen (ie mere-hen, with the common confusion of -moor and -mere) is no doubt implied. The modern word 'cock' is derived from OE *cocc*, giving place-names like Cockey La, in which the second element was *gehæg*, 'enclosure', and Coquet Nb with *wudu*, 'wood'. The compound *cocc-scīete*, meaning 'a woodland glade where nets were set to trap woodcock', is the origin of numerous minor names such as Cockshoot Gl, He, O, Sr, Wa, Wo, YW and variants such as Cockshutt(s) Db, Nt, YW. The female bird, OE *henn*, enters seldom into the naming of places. It is the first element of

Henley Sa, but most Henleys (O, Sf, So, Sr, Wa) were 'at the high (*hēan*, dative) wood (*lēah*)'. OE *henn* is combined with *þyrne*, a mutated form of *þorn*, 'thorntree', in Henthorn La and with *riđ*, 'stream', in Hendred, Brk.

FISHES

As would be expected, place-names involving words for fish (OE *fisc*) commonly refer to water, as in Fishbourne Sx, Wt, Fishlake YW, with *lacu*, 'stream' and Fishwick La. In this last name, *wīc* implies a building devoted to a particular occupation, probably the curing of fish.

The eel (OE *ǣl*, ON *ál*) is the descriptive element in Alford L, Elham K (*hām*), Auburn YE and Ely C. The second element of Ely was OE *gē*, a word which became disused early in the Anglo-Saxon period. It meant 'district' and recurs in the name Surrey, which was the 'southern district' in relation to Middlesex. Eastry K, 'eastern district' and Vange Ess, which in a tenth-century document is spelt *Fengge*, 'fen district', are further instances of its use.

In Mortlake Sr (*lacu*), Morte Point and Morthoe D (*hōh*, 'headland'), we have the word *mort*, which is likely to have meant 'a young salmon'; but a personal name *Mort(a)* cannot be ruled out in these names.

INSECTS

The bee (OE *bēo*), probably because of its economic value, is of common occurrence in place-names, as in Beoley Wo, Bewick Nb, YE, in the latter of which we have a use of *wīc* comparable to that in Fishwick above. The enclosure (*worđ*) of Beauworth Ha may have been an earthwork similar to the undated enclosure called the Bee Garden on Chobham Common, Sr, which, surmounted by hurdles, would have protected the hives from the wind. A field-name Beegarden is recorded from the early seventeenth century in Gloucestershire.

Beckett Brk is a compound of *bēo* with *cot*, 'hut, cottage' and may be the source of the surname Beckett. But it may have other origins, the most likely being exemplified by a Devonshire place-name that goes back to OE *Biccancot(e)*, 'Bicca's cottage'. Betchett's Green Sr is derived from OE *bēc-ett*, 'beech-copse', but this, too, could give rise to a modern form Beckett. Similarly, the surname and place-name Birchett Ess (etc) was *bircet(t)*, 'birch-copse'; Chislett K and the identical surname are from *cistelet(t)*, 'chestnut-copse'; and several disused minor names *Haselett(e)* Ess, Sr, W of the thirteenth and fourteenth centuries, from *hæslet(t)*, 'hazel-copse' are the origin of the surname. The family of William Hazlitt, the essayist, very probably took its name from Haselette in the parish of Winterbourne Gunner W.

The humble-bee (*dora*) is represented by Dorney Bk, with the ending *ēg*, 'island'; and honey is referred to in Honeybourne Gl, Wo, where the colour of the water must be meant. Honiton D was a 'honey (*hunig*)-farm (*tūn*)'.

Wigley Db, Ha and Wigwell Db contain either the personal name *Wicga* or the Old English word for a beetle, which was *wigga*. This survives in the insect-name 'earwig' and the related verb 'wiggle', and in all of these words the root idea is 'to move'. It is interesting to note that the verbs 'weigh', 'wag', 'waggle', and the nouns 'wain' and 'wagon', are also related and that the same root occurs in Latin *vehere* and its derivative *vehiculum*. From this we may see that the words 'vehicle' and 'wagon' share the same Indo-Germanic root syllable as well as retaining a relationship of meaning.

The ephemeral insects occur in Gnatham Co, D, where *gnætt* is combined with *hamm*, 'water-meadow', a common habitat of gnats on the wing; and *stūt*, which had the same meaning, is found in Stuchbury Nth, probably as a personal name, the whole meaning '*Stūt*'s fort (*burh*)'; and in Stuston Sf, where it can hardly mean other than '*Stūt*'s farm'; Midgeham Brk, with *hām*, 'homestead' and Midgley YW have OE *mycg*, 'midge, gnat'.

One of the most destructive insects is the weevil (OE *wifel*), but pest though it is and was, its name was applied to persons, as in

31

Wilsthorpe Db, L, YE, YW, with ON *þorp*, 'outlying farm', though the insect may have been intended in Wilsford L, W. The corn weevil (OE *hamstra*) must have abounded in an arable clearing (*lēah*) at Hamsterley Du.

Among the lowly forms of life that had significance for our ancestors was the leech (*lǣce*), one of the annelid worms which sucks blood from animals, including man. The twenty-six or so British species were lumped together under the one name, though only one was probably used for controlled blood-letting in medicine. *Lǣce* is probably the origin of the first element of Latchmere Sr—a pond from which leeches were obtained; and of Lashbrook C. Certainty is difficult because of confusion with the word *lǣc(c)*, 'stream, bog', which is the natural habitat of the leech. The Latchmoors or -mores (both with -*mere*, 'pool'), frequent as a minor name in southern counties, probably contain *lǣc(c)*, as do Latchford Ch, Latchley Co and the Gloucestershire river-name Leach, beside which are situated Eastleach, Northleach and Lechlade (with (*ge*-)*lād*), 'a river-crossing'). Another similar word *lǣce*, 'a physician', is found in Lesbury Nb and Lexham Nf.

EXTINCT ANIMALS

There has been a steady decline in the number of species able to co-exist with man and his many disturbing activities. The destruction of the forests to create pasture and arable, the drainage of the fens and marshes and of the river valleys, the spread of domestic grazing animals and the presence of man himself—all these and other factors have caused gradual changes in habitat tending to sharpen the competition between man and wild beasts; and always to the disadvantage, and sometimes to the final doom, of the animals.

The beaver (OE *beofor*) was among the first to die out. Its habit of creating lakes by damming rivers rendered considerable areas almost useless for any human purpose; and for this reason alone it would have been persecuted. The value of its fur for clothes and of its flesh for food condemned it to extinction in the ninth century, by which time Anglo-Saxon colonisation had begun to spread out from its original settlements areas. In most place-names, the word *beofor* is combined with a word for stream, as in Barbourne Wo, Beverley YE (with (*lic(c)*, 'stream') and Beversbrook W. Beverley (Brook) Sr and Beverley YW, both with *lēah*, indicate its woodland haunts and Bevercotes Nt might be thought to mean 'beaver-lodges', except that the European beaver, unlike the American, lives in tunnels burrowed into river-banks. If the first element is not a personal name *Beofor*, it is likely that the cottages were built near a beaver colony.

The bear is also said to have survived in England until the ninth century, though there are no certain references to it in place-names. Its Old English name *bera* is probably used as a personal name in Barbury W, an Iron Age hill-fort (*burh*) and, more certainly, in Barham K. Barford Bd may contain the same name, but most Barfords (eg O, Wa, W) have the meaning 'ford which can carry a load of corn or barley (*bere*)'.

It was not until the late fifteenth century that the last wolf was killed in England, though, like other animals, it survived longer in the more remote regions of Great Britain which were sparsely inhabited. The word *wulf* was used, as one would expect, as a personal name, but where it is combined with natural features of the landscape, such as lakes, woods and valleys, the animal-name is likely. Although a denizen of the forest, the wolf emerged on the fringes of habitable areas to attack flocks and herds, but seldom adult humans. Some kind of defence (*weard*) against their attacks is implied by Wolford Wa; and it may be traced still as a partly surviving earthwork surrounding the village of Great Wolford. A palisade built upon it would have afforded efficient protection against the marauders from the nearby forest, of which a large fragment still exists as Wolford Wood. A similar defensive work may have existed at Wolfage Nth, in which the word 'hedge' (*hecg*) must imply something more substantial than a hedge as we now understand it. Wolvey

Wa (*wulf-hege*) contains a related word meaning 'hedge or fence'.

The animal-name is combined with words for valley in Woldale YW (*dæl*) and Woolden La (*denu*) and with *lēah*, 'woodland', in Woolley Brk, Hu, YW. Woolmer Ha was originally the name of the pond (*mere*) which is still a feature of the area. In the Danelaw, *wulf* interchanges with ON *úlfr* in names such as Owlands YN (with *lūndr*, 'a small wood') and Ulpha Cu (with *haugr*, 'hill, burial mound'). The minor name Woolpit Gl, Sf, Ess, Db, YW, was originally *Wulf-pytt* and provides a clue to one of the methods of extermination of the pest. Yet another word, ON *vargr* (cognate with OE *wearg*, 'a criminal or outlaw', see p 127) may refer to the wolf or to a human outcast and occurs in Wragholme L, combined with ON *holmr*, 'an island', as well as in Wraggmire Cu, with ON *mýrr*, 'a bog'.

A dangerous beast if encountered, but otherwise not a serious problem to primitive farming communities, was the wild boar. Whether wild or domestic, it was *bār* in Old English. It fed in the woods, hence Barley La and Barlow Db, both with *lēah*. In Barsham Nf, Sf we have compounds with *hām*, 'homestead', and would expect a personal name, but in Bosworth Lei, even though the first element is in the genitive singular(-'s), we may have reference to a 'boar-enclosure (*worð*)'. Another word for boar, OE *eofor*, was probably restricted in usage to the wild animal. Its ferocity made it a suitable emblem for wearing on the battle helmet to strike fear into the heart of the enemy. This custom is mentioned in the Beowulf poem; and two tiny boars' heads decorate the helmet found in the tomb of an East Anglian prince at Sutton Hoo, Suffolk. This was a magnificent ship-burial under a large barrow, containing a great number of royal treasures but no certain trace of a body. This word *eofor* occurs in the place-names Everton Bd, La, Nt and Everley W, YN. In Eversley Ha, with a genitive singular -'s, it was a personal name. It is said that the last English boar was killed in Staffordshire at the end of the seventeenth century. Certainly it was still being hunted in Windsor Forest, Brk in 1617.

The wild cat survived in England to the early nineteenth century. In place-names OE *cat(t)* may refer to the wild or domestic animal or it may be a personal name. In Catley C, He, L and in Catcleugh Nb (with *clōh*, 'a ravine'), the wild cat is likely; in Catford Lo we may have a personal name.

The few herds of wild cattle that still survive, as at Chillingham Nb, have been crossed somewhat with domestic varieties. They were probably introduced from the Continent, perhaps during the Roman period. Their ancestors, or just possibly the European bison, were known to the Anglo-Saxons as *ūr*, a word that survives in Urpeth Du, meaning 'cattle-path (*pæð*)' and Urswick La, 'farm (*wīc*) by the cattle (*ūr*)-lake (*sǣ*)'. ON *úrr*, 'a kind of ox', cognate with the Old English word, is unlikely as an alternative to it in these place-names.

CHAPTER 3

Plants, Grasses and Trees

Village communities living perilously from year to year at a bare subsistence level had to be most careful about what land they chose for their crops. A bad choice might mean failure of the harvest at irregular intervals and this would have meant famine and death for many. If the crops of one village failed, it was likely that its neighbours too were suffering from a dearth of food. *The Anglo-Saxon Chronicle* records disastrous famine (*se mycla hungor*, 'the great hunger') in AD 793, 975, 1005, 1044, 1082, 1087, 1096, 1124 and 1125. These were national disasters (*geond Angel cynn*, 'throughout England'); local failures of crops were not recorded, even though many peasants died. Murrain among cattle is noted in the *Chronicle* on nine occasions; and throughout the Saxon and earlier medieval period large areas were from time to time laid waste by marauding armies of Angles, Saxons, Danes, Norwegians and Normans. Wars between the Anglo-Saxon kingdoms and invasions by the Northmen occurred successively, with few lengthy intervals of peace. For men and women in every rank of society, existence was constantly threatened by famine, disease and war.

Yet the population tended to expand and new land had to be broken in for cultivation as an insurance against hunger (see p 90 f). Choice of land in the first place was possible merely by noting the vegetation it naturally supported. Plant communities afford information concerning permeability—whether the soil is well drained or not—and its alkalinity or acidity. The digging of a hole could be far less informative and far more laborious with primitive implements.

The earliest English settlers could take over the fields of their sub-Roman predecessors and even in regions where agriculture had declined, the scrub-invaded fields were easier to clear than virgin land. Moreover, the Romano–Britons had tilled the best soils in the valleys as well as on the uplands and their successors were wise to use their dwelling-sites and their fields, even where they had been for long deserted. They seldom took over upland sites, but it is probable that the old valley settlements and fields were the first they chose to occupy, rather than virgin land.

The plant-names that occur in place-names total several dozen and only a selection of the important or more interesting ones is possible. Among these are words for crops, of which cereals were by far the most important in the Saxon economy. Barley (*bere*) was a widespread crop. Farms mainly producing it (*bere-tūn*) were numerous and their names often survive as Barton. This is found in all but eight of the English counties. OE *bere-wīc*, of similar meaning, occurs as Berwick, a very common name, or Barwick Co, YW and Borwick La. A storehouse for barley, or for corn of other kinds, *bere-ærn*, gives us the word 'barn' and place-names such as Barn(e)s Nb, Sr and Barnfield K. The name Barford was briefly considered earlier (p 33).

Place-names suggest that wheat (OE *hwǣte*, ON *hveiti*) was a common crop also. W(h)addon Brk, W, Wo were named from hills (*dūn*) on which it was grown. Wheathill Sa, So (with *hyll*), Whatborough Lei and Whiteborough Nt (with *beorg*) had a similar meaning. The numerous Wheatleys were clearings (*lēah*) and Wheatacre Nf, Whiteacre K were plots of arable (*æcer*) where this crop was grown.

Rye, which will give fair returns on soils that other cereals would not tolerate, provided the grain for the dark bread which was the staple food of peasants over much of northern Europe. Ryton Du, Sa, Wa, Royton La and Ruyton Sa were farms where rye (*rȳge*) was commonly grown. Ryhill YE, YW needs no explanation but Roydon Ess, Sf was the hill (*dūn*) growing with rye (*rȳgen*), an adjectival derivative of the crop-name. Roughton L, Nf may contain the cognate ON *rúgr*, or possibly OE *rūh*, 'rough'.

Oats, which today are a crop mainly of northern counties, find no mention in the place-names of the south midland or southern counties that have been studied so far by the English Place-Name Society, though absence from place-names is no proof that this crop was never grown in the south. Harborough Lei is a compound of OE *hæfera*, 'oats' and *beorg*, 'hill'; Haverhill Sf has the same meaning whereas Haverigg Cu, La is from ON *hafri* and ON *hryggr*, 'ridge', but has the same general connotation.

Fodder crops, such as clover (OE *clæfre*), were almost as important as cereals for human survival and words for them occur quite frequently in place-names. Claverton Ch was a farm in some way characterised by clover and Claverdon St, Wa a hill (*dūn*) where it was grown. Cabbage or kale (OE *cāl*), food for men or cattle, was a speciality of a farm (*wīc*) that was the original nucleus of the settlement at Colwich St and Colworth Bd was 'an enclosure, homestead or village (*worð*)' where it was cultivated. Cress (OE *cærse*) is a word found usually with endings indicating the growth of the plant in water as, for instance, Carswell Brk, Gl, Caswell Do, Nth, Creswell Db, Nb, St, Kerswell D, Wo, all of which contain *-wella*, 'spring, stream'; and Crisbrook K, Kersbrook Co, had a similar meaning; Kersey Sf was an island (*ēg*) where cress grew. Peasmarsh Sx and Pusey Brk refer to peas (OE *pise*), the latter name also originally ending in *ēg*; and a crop of value as a source of dye was woad (*wād*), which either grew naturally or was purposely cultivated at Waddon Do, Sr (with *dūn*). At Watton Hrt there was a farm (*tūn*) that specialised in producing the dye. Croydon, near Waddon Sr, was the 'saffron (*croh*) valley (*denu*)', that is, a place where the autumn crocus (*Colchicum autumnale*) grew. This plant was valued as a source of yellow colouring-matter and of colchicine, a medicinal drug.

38

GRASSES

There are about twenty different words for grasses and related plants, some of them of rare occurrence except locally in minor names. The British climate is well suited for the production of good greensward, yet it is not a natural feature of our landscape but the result of countless generations of human effort, conscious and unconscious, as well as of the grazing of domestic animals. The greater part of lowland England was high forest until man began to disturb the natural ecological balance of plant and animal communities and, left to itself, it would re-revert to its primeval wooded state. Grassland that is ungrazed and otherwise untended will revert to scrub and eventually to woodland, with most kinds of grasses suppressed by the competition of more dominant plants. The agricultural depression of the inter-war years resulted in such neglect, and thorn-scrub especially was to be seen invading many a pasture both on the uplands and in the valleys. Here and there even forest trees, oak and elm in particular, were gaining a foothold, only to be swept away by the intensive ploughing of the war years.

Between 150 and 160 species of grass are native to Britain and their distribution is largely determined by soil and climatic conditions. It is difficult to correlate botanical species with the Old English and Old Norse names, though some broad groups are identifiable. Those characteristic of damp situations, such as the reeds (OE *hrēod*) usually occur in place-names with endings descriptive of water, such as Radbourn(e) Db, Wa, Redbourn Hrt, L (with *burna*, 'stream') or Radipole Do (with *pōl*, 'pool'). Ridley Ess, K has the same word in the first syllable and *lēah*, 'wood or clearing' as the second, whereas Ridley Ch, Nb have *rȳd*, 'cleared or rid (of trees)' as first element.

Another term for reed was OE *bune*, which is difficult to distinguish from the personal name *Buna* in, for instance, Bumpstead Ess, of which the final syllable was *stede*, 'a place'; but in Bunny

Nf we have the readily intelligible 'reed-island (*ēg*)', and in Bunwell Nf the reeds grew beside a spring or stream (*wella*). The closely allied rush-plants are represented by several words, of which OE *rysc* is the commonest. In Rushton, a frequent place-name, it is combined with *tūn* and in Rishworth YW with *worð*, 'enclosure, farm'. In Rushett(s) K, Sr, Sx we have the derivative *ryscett*, 'a rush-bed, a place of rushes' and in Rushwick Wo another derived word *rixuc*, with the same meaning. And sedges (OE *secg*), grow in similar damp places, giving such names as Sedgemoor So and Sedgewick Sx, though one cannot be sure that the latter name does not contain OE *secg*, 'a warrior' or *Secg* a personal name. It would be more normal for a habitative terminal such as *wīc*, 'a dwelling or building for special purposes', to have a personal name or a word for a human being, the owner, as first element. The Old Norse word *sef* gives Seathwaite Cu, 'clearing (*þveit*) with sedge', in a locality which has the greatest rainfall in England and so conducive to moisture-loving plants. Sefton La has the same word.

The bent-grasses, seven species of *agrostis*, range in their distribution from dry heaths to wet ditches, according to the kind. In Bentham Gl, YW we have OE *beonet* combined with *hām*, 'homestead'; and in the frequently-recurring Bentley the same word occurs with *lēah*, here meaning 'a clearing' rather than 'a wood'. With the same meaning, OE *bēos* occurs in Be(e)sthorpe L, Nt and Beeston Nf, Nt, St, YW, all of which are originally settlement-names with either ON *þorp*, 'dependent farmstead etc' or OE *tūn*, 'farmstead etc'. The ON *stǫrr*, 'bent-grass' or 'sedge', is the origin of the first element in Starbeck YW, with ON *bekkr*, 'brook' and Stargill Cu, a compound with the Old West Scandinavian word *gil*, 'a ravine'.

Another mainly North Country name is Snape(s) La, YE, YN, YW and its compounds such as Bulsnape and Kidsnape, both with obvious animal prefixes. It appears to go back to an Icelandic word *snap*, meaning 'poor pasture'. ('Snape' with a quite different origin is discussed later, p 74.) And OE *feax*, literally 'hair', was used in a metaphorical sense of 'rough grass' in, for

40

instance, Halifax YW (with OE *hall*, 'a slope') or in Faxton Nth (with *tūn*).

The strange names Fitts YN, YW and (The) Fitz or Coldfitz Cu contain ON *fit*, 'grassland on the bank of a river'; and OE *fogga*, from which is derived the modern name of a grass, Yorkshire Fog (*Holcus lanatus*), is the origin of the first element of Foggithwaite Cu. Clumps of coarse grass (OE *hassuc*) gave their name to Hezicar YW (with ON *kjarr*, 'marsh'); and Hassocks is a common field-name in C, Nt, Nth, Db. The Sussex place also originated as a field-name. The euphonious Hautbois Nf contains another OE word for a clump of grass, namely *hobbe*; the modern syllable 'bois' has undergone a strange transformation from the original OE *wisse*, 'meadow, marsh'.

The generic word OE *gærs, græs, gres*, ON *gres*, appears frequently as an element in names on the map of England. Garsdon W (with *dūn*), Grasmere We, still an apt description of the lake, and Gresham Nf (*hām*) are varied instances. Gresgarth La (with ON *garðr*, 'an enclosure') and Grassthorpe Nt (with ON *þorp*, 'a dependent farm'), may have ON *gres* rather than the OE word with the same form. OE *gærsen*, 'growing with grass' or OE *gærsing*, 'grazing, pasture' are difficult to distinguish in Garsington O, Grassendale La, Grassington YW and Gressingham La. A paddock, OE *gærs-tūn*, literally 'grass-enclosure', is the source of Garston Ha, Hrt and Woodgarston Ha.

Dried grass (OE *hēg*), is the meaning of the first syllable of Hailey Hrt, O, Haydon Do, Nb, So (*dūn*), Hayton Cu, Nt, Sa (*tūn*), Hayford Nth, O and many more. The very common occurrence of this word 'hay' reflects its vital importance as winter fodder. OE *hēg* is sometimes confused in medieval records of place-names with (*ge-*)*hæg*, 'an enclosure' and *hege*, 'a fence or hedge'. (See p 79.)

TREES

The correspondence between the Old English names for trees is almost complete. Most of the native species are represented, although one cannot distinguish between the two species of common oak, sessile and pedunculate, or between the dozen willow species that attain the normal height of trees.

Places named from the presence of the oak (OE *āc*) are as widespread as the modern distribution of this tree. The common name Acton and, of the same derivation, Aughton La, YE, numerous Oakleys, Acomb Nb, YN, YW (OE dative plural *ācum*, 'at the oaks') and Matlock Db, 'oak where the moot (OE *mæðel*, 'speech') was held', represent only a few of the many place-names containing *āc*. ON *eik* was the origin of the first syllable of Aigburth La (with ON *berg*, 'hill') and Aysgarth YN (with ON *skarð*), the whole name meaning 'pass marked by an oak'.

The elm (OE *elm*) was characteristic of the place called Elmley K, Wo (*lēah*, 'a wood'), Elmham Nf (*hām*, 'homestead'), and Elmstead Ess, K (*stede*, 'a place'); and the wych-elm marked a river-crossing at Wishford W and was grey (*hār*) with lichen at Horwich La. This is a tree distinctive of the valleys which, in their dampest stretches, especially beside the rivers, abound still in willows (OE *wilig*). Wilby Nf, Nth, Sf, Willoughby L, Lei, Nt, Wa—both compounds with ON *bý*, 'farm'—and Willey Ch, He (with *lēah*) are derived from this word. The related *wilign* gives Willington Bd, Db. Other Willingtons have personal names: the one in Cheshire was '*Wynflæd*'s farm' (a woman's name); those in County Durham and Northumberland were 'farm of *Wifel*'s people' and the Warwickshire one was the farm of '*Wulflāf*'s people'. OE *welig*, a variant of *wilig* and meaning the same, is the origin of the first element of Welford Brk; and it occurs in the dative plural as Welwyn Hrt, 'at the willows'.

The modern word 'withy' (OE *wīðig*) is obvious in Withycombe D, So and Withypool So and at this place there are still willows besides a broadening of the River Barle (OE *pōl*). This use of the word 'pool' is similar to that in the phrase 'Pool of London', which describes the reach of the Thames immediately below Tower Bridge. *Wīðig* was the first syllable of Widford Ess, Hrt, O and Weeton La, YW also. There can be little doubt that this

Old English word was applied to *Salix viminalis* ('the weaving willow'), usually known since the Middle Ages as the 'osier', a word borrowed from Old French and meaning ultimately 'a willow bed'. Plantings of osiers had great economic importance as a source of the main material used in basketry and wicker-work.

Yet another kind of willow is represented by OE *salh*, which is clearly related to the Latin *salix* and had the same meaning. It is also the origin of our word 'sallow', used of *S. caprea*, the goat willow and the grey (*S. cinerea*) and eared (*S. aurita*) sallows. The grey is the commonest and most widely distributed of our willows. One or other of these species is referred to in Salford Bd, La, Wo, in Sale Ch and Zeals W. Salford Priors Wa, a manor held by Kenilworth Priory from AD 1122, was 'the salt (OE *salt*) ford', so named because it was situated on one of the tracks along which salt was transported from the Droitwich area; but Saltley Wa is from *saliht*, 'growing with willows' and another related word *sele*, 'willow copse', explains the first syllable of Selborne Ha (with *burna*), Selworthy So (with *worðig*, 'enclosure'), and Silchester Ha. The final element, *ceaster*, of this last name refers to the Romano-British town and tribal centre, of which the walls still survive. The ON *selja*, 'a willow', cognate with OE *salh*, gives Selby YW and Selside We, YW, the latter originally ending in ON *sætr*, 'mountain pasture or shieling'. (See p 115.)

The aspen (OE *æspe, æpse*), a tree of moist but light soils, commonly occurs today in small groups, but apparently in earlier times it formed woods (*lēah*); hence the names Apsley Bk, Wa and Aspley Bd, Nt, St. Another tree of damp places, the alder (OE *alor*) is represented by Alresford Ha, Aldershaw St (with *sceaga*, 'copse'), and Ollerton La, Nt (with *tūn*). The related word *alren*, 'growing with alders', is found in Ollerenshaw Db. These last two place-names show a development of the 'a' of *alor* to 'o' which is characteristic of the West and North Midlands. The cognate ON *elri*, 'alder tree or alderwood', occurs in Ellerbeck Cu, La, YW and in Ellerton YW, YN. The elder (OE

43

ellern) is another common tree and the word is of wide distribution as in Elste(a)d Sf, Sr and Elstob Du (*stubb*, 'tree-stump') and another OE word, *hyldre*, was used of the same tree, giving Ilderton Nb and Hinderclay Sf, which is terminated by the rare word *clā*, meaning 'claw-like' or 'cloven' and must have referred to a tree with a split trunk. Even more common, the hawthorn (OE *hagu-þorn*) gives rise to such names as Hatherleigh D (with *lēah*) and Hatherton St (originally with *dūn*, 'hill'). Its fruit, the haw (OE *hagga*), or a personal name *Hæcga*, is referred to in the first syllable of the common place-name Hagley Sa, So, St.

Commonest of all tree-names on the map is OE *þorn*, 'a thorn tree', a plant much used then as now for hedging. This is its significance in the frequent name Thornton, which was 'an enclosure (*tūn*) protected with thorns'; and much the same may have been true of Thornbrough Nb, YW and Thornbury Gl, He (all with *burh*, 'stronghold') and with Thorney Nt, Thornhaugh Nth (both with OE *haga*, 'hedge' or 'enclosure'). Thorney C, Mx, So, Sx, 'thorn-island (*ēg*)'; Thor(n)ley Du, Hrt, Wt, 'thorn-wood'; Thornham K, La, Nf, Sf, 'homestead (*hām*) among thorn trees'; Thornhill Db, Do, W, YW and Thorne Co, K, So, YW, 'at the thorn tree' are varied instances of its widespread use. And a variant, OE *þyrne* or ON *þyrnir* or even an Old East Scandinavian personal name *Pyrni* is found in names like Thrimby We (ON *bý*, 'farm' or 'village') and Thornham La, which was a dative plural, 'at the thorn trees'.

On well-drained soils, the ash tree is often dominant and it figures in many place-names, especially those of localties on limestone or chalk. Ashton or, in the Danelaw, Ashby, are common and in its ON form *askr*, the tree-name is found in Askrigg YN (with OE *ric*, 'a narrow strip'), in Askwith YW, meaning 'ash wood' (ON *viðr*) and in Askern YN (with OE *ærn*, 'house'). The related ON *eski*, 'place overgrown with ash trees', is the first element of Eastoft L, YW (with ON *topt*, 'a curtilage'), Escrick YE (*ric*) and Hesket Cu, 'a headland (OE *hēafod*) overgrown with ash trees'. Even more typical of the chalk and limestone uplands is the beech (OE *bēce*). In its uncompounded form this word is found as Beech Brk, St or, further north, in a compound, Beckwith YW, in which OE *wudu* has been replaced by ON *viðr*, both meaning 'wood'. In its unmutated form *bōc* we have Bookham Sr (with *hām*), Buckhurst Ess, K, Sx ('beech-wood hill'), Buckholt Gl, Ha, K (with *holt*, 'a wood'), and possibly Boughton Ch, K. But this same word *bōc* came to mean 'book, charter'—that is, something written—for it seems that the earliest 'paper' was beech-board on which writing was incised. The earliest surviving Anglo-Saxon writings are in the runic alphabet, one that was evolved for carving in wood. By the ninth century, this form of writing had been completely replaced by the Roman alphabet written in ink on parchment. However, the very common place-name Buckland meant 'land (granted by) charter (*bōc*)'. This was a form of tenure distinct from *folc-land*, which was land from which the king drew food-rents and customary services. Faulkland So and Falklands Wo are among the rare instances of such a tenure of which the memory is preserved in place-names. *Bōc-land* was held free of these services and possibly the farms, Boughton Ch, K were similarly held and not named from beech-trees.

In similar situations to those of beech and ash, but where the soil tends to be acid, especially on heathlands, the birch (OE *beorc*) dominates the plant community. Bartlet Ha, Wo, Berk(e)-ley Gl, So were birchwoods (*lēah*) and Berkhamsted Hrt was a homestead established near or among these trees. The OE word *birce*, a related form, and the cognate ON *birki* are difficult to distinguish, but one or other of them occurs in Birchover Db, meaning '(river-)bank (OE *ōfer*) overgrown with birches' and in Birchills St. In Birkenhead Ch, Birkenshaw YW (with *sceaga*, 'wood') and Birkenside Nb we have the adjective OE *bircen*, so that the first and last of these names meant headland (OE *hēafod*) and 'hillside (OE *sīde*) overgrown with birches'.

A tree of former economic importance, the lime (OE *lind*), gave bast from its inner bark for rope-making and timber for the construction of war-shields. The large-leaved lime, *Tilia platyphyllos*, which is probably the only native species, is now

45

limited as a wild tree to Herefordshire and the West Riding, though in earlier times it had a much wider distribution, as place-names show. At Lindhurst and Lyndhurst Ha, K, Nt it formed copses (OE *hyrst*) and whole woods of them existed at Lindley YW and Linwood Ha, L. Lindrick Nt, YW were places characterised by narrow strips (OE *ric*) of such woodland and at Lindridge K, Wo, lime-trees grew on a ridge (OE *hrycg*). The place-name Lindfield Sx means 'open country (*feld*) with lime-trees'.

Our only native maple (OE *mapel, mapuldor*) does not form dense stands and is commonly found in isolation or in small groups. The absence of this tree-name, in combination with words for 'wood' suggests that a sparse but wide distribution existed in earlier times. In Mappleton Db, YE this tree gave name to a farm (*tūn*) and in Mapledurham Ha, O there was a homestead (*hām*) beside which a maple (*mapuldor*) grew. Mappowder Do is derived from this form, but without any addition.

Of smaller trees, the box (OE *box*), affords a close-grained hard wood which was at one time of value in the making of containers and, in more recent centuries, provided the engraver with his best material. The tree is sometimes said to have been introduced by the Romans; others believe it to be a true native. It occurs abundantly at Boxhill Sr and on the Chilterns. A large stand existed formerly at Boxley K and another remains still at Boxwell, Gl. The names Box Gl, Hrt, W, Boxford Brk, Sf, Boscombe W, and Boxgrove Sx all occur on chalk, limestone or other calcareous soils which are necessary for the growth of this tree. The same is true of Bexhill Sx, Bexley K and Bix O, all of which are derived from the related word *byxe*, or *bexe* in its Kentish form.

Our most abundant evergreen tree, the holly (OE *holegn*) is the source of the name Holme YW and Holne D (but see p 66 for another derivation of some names in -holme or Holme); and there are many Hollywoods in the category of minor place-names. It may have been planted in early times to provide a timber that could be used as a substitute for the scarcer box, as it has many of the virtues of the latter when worked.

It is sometimes said that the Scots Pine (OE *sæppe*) became extinct in southern Britain and that its modern occurrence is due to deliberate planting. This is, however, very unlikely in view of the finding of charred pine-wood in Wiltshire in a later prehistoric occupation level and other evidence from more recent times. The word is, nevertheless, absent from southern places apart from Sabden So (and also La), where it is combined with *denu*, 'a valley'. At Sapley Hu, in the Midlands, there was a sufficient number of pines to form a wood (*lēah*).

The common word for tree was OE *trēow* and it survives in a variety of compound place-names. Trowbridge W and Langtree D, La are obvious in their meanings, but Trewyn D had a weak nominative plural in -*en*, 'the trees'; Aintree La has as first syllable ON *einn*, 'one, solitary' and Manningtree Ess has OE *manig*, 'many'. Coventry Wa, with the personal name *Cofa* and Oswestry Sa, with *Ōswald*, are representative of many such compounds. The Shropshire name referred to a *rōd-trēow*, 'a holy cross', commemorative of St Oswald, the revered king of the Northumbrians. The second syllable of the modern word 'hornbeam' retains the OE word *bēam* in the sense 'tree'. It was used, too, of a tree-trunk which, carpentered, became 'a beam'. Bampton Cu, O, We meant either 'farm built of beams' or 'farm by a (prominent) tree'. Holbeam D, K presumably described 'a tree in a hollow (OE *hol*) and Benfleet Ess, 'an inlet (*flēot*) bridged by beams or trees'. The latter meaning would be close to that of Trowbridge, above. The word *timber* could also mean 'trees, timber', as it still does; and in the form (*ge-*) *timbre* it could connote 'a building'. At Timsbury Ha, a fort (*burh*) was constructed of timber and at Timperleigh Ch there was a wood which was no doubt cropped for timber.

Several words for 'wood' or 'copse' have already occurred in a number of compound place-names, but something more must be said of them to indicate such distinctions of meaning as may be made between them. A forest (OE *wald* in the Anglian dialects,

47

weald in Kentish and West Saxon) was the most extensive tract of woodland; The Weald of the South-East extended into three counties. But lesser tracts are probably implied by Weald Bk, Ess, Hu, O and in Waltham Brk, Ess, Ha, K, Lei, L, Sx, a compound with *hām*. The Anglian form *wald* gives names such as Southwold Sf, Northwold Nf and Prestwold La, the last of these names being 'priest (OE *prēost*) -wood'. The word 'wold', however, came to mean 'upland' even though the region were treeless, but it is likely that the Cotswolds (with the personal name *Cōd*), the Yorkshire and the Lincolnshire wolds were wooded in early Saxon times and that, when first applied to these uplands, *wald* meant 'forest'.

OE *lēah*, which has already appeared in many of the preceding paragraphs, could be applied to an extensive forest such as The Weald. In the late ninth century it was called *Andredes leage* as well as *Andredes weald*. *Andred* was the Celtic name for the Roman fort at the place later called by the Saxons Pevensey (*Pefen*'s island [*ēg*].) There is a good deal of evidence to show that *lēah* originally meant 'forest' and later 'a clearing in a forest'. Much later still, it came to mean 'a field' through confusion with *lǣs*, 'a meadow'. In most place-names, *lēah* probably meant 'a woodland glade', that is, a natural clearing; but the word with which it is linked may imply more clearly that, in the particular instance, it referred to either 'woodland' or to 'a clearing' within it. With tree-names such as Oakley, Ashley, Elmley, Thornley or Willey, a wood is likely. With crop-names like Flaxley, Lindley or Wheatley there must have been a clearing in which the crops were grown. However, names such as Lea L, Lee Bk, Ess, Ha, K, Sa or the very frequent Leigh, were probably given in the century or so after the Norman Conquest when the final meaning of 'meadow' had come into use.

OE *wudu*, 'a wood', and its ON cognate *viðr*, have also been exemplified many times; and so has OE *sceaga*, 'a copse or shaw'; but the ON cognate of the latter word, *skógr*, 'a wood', has not yet appeared. Askew YN was 'an oak (ON *eik*) wood' and Swinscoe St was one where pigs (OE *swīn*) were pastured. Briscoe Cu was woodland associated in some way with Britons (OE *Brettas*) and Scaws, Sceugh and Schoose Cu were 'woods' without a descriptive addition.

A smaller stand of trees, 'a copse' or 'wooded hill' (OE *hyrst*), is relatively common in place-names. In its simple form as Hirst Nb, YW or Hurst, in widespread instances, it is to be found all over England. The Sussex names Herstmonceux and Hurstpierpoint have the family names of medieval manorial lords affixed. Chislehurst K (OE *ceosol*, 'gravel'), Sandhurst Brk, Gl, K (OE *sand*) and Stonyhurst La (OE *stānig*) describe the soil of the wood; Deerhurst Gl (OE *dēor*, see p 22), Lamberhurst K (OE *lamb*) and Hawkhurst K (OE *hafoc*, 'a hawk') refer to the creatures inhabiting it; and the trees of which it was composed are specified in Ashurst Ha, K, La, Sx, Ewhurst Ha, Sr, Sx (OE *īw*, 'yew') and Nuthurst La, Wa (OE *hnutu*).

Rare in the North but common elsewhere is OE *holt*, 'a wood, a thicket'. Uncompounded as modern Holt, it is quite frequent and it occurs in compounds such as Occold Sf (*āc*, 'oak') and Buckholt Ha, K (*bōc*, 'beech'). OE *fyrhð(e)* is similar in meaning to *holt*, though it may sometimes refer to a more extensive tract of woodland. It occurs on the modern map as Frith La, Mx (Chapel en le) Frith Db, and Thrift K, Ess, Nth, Wo, Sr etc, often with the tautological addition of 'Wood'. Firbank We (ME *bank*, 'slope of a hill'), Frithsden Hrt (*denu*, 'valley') and Pirbright Sr (OE *pirige*, 'pear tree') are fairly typical compounds with this word.

The modern 'grove' is derived from OE *grāf(a)*. The many Graftons were farms near a grove of trees; and Graf(f)ham Hu, Sx was a *hām*, 'homestead', similarly situated. By itself, 'Grove' is common and so is the compound 'Groveland(s)'. OE *bearu* had much the same meaning as *grāf(a)* and survives as Beer Co, D, Bere D, Do and Bare Db. It has sometimes developed to Barrow Db, La, So, which is the normal modern form of OE *beorg*, 'hill, burial mound, barrow'. In the Danelaw, ON *lúndr* was commonly used of 'a small wood, a grove', including some that had pagan religious associations. Lound L, Nt, Sf, Lund, YE, YN,

YW and Lunt La represent the simple form of this word. As a final element it was confused with OE *land* and occurs in such names as Shrubland Sf, Timberland L, Kirkland La (ON *kirkja*, 'church'), Morland We (OE *mōr*, 'moor'), Holland Hu (ON *hagi*, 'an enclosure') and Rowlands Db, which is either from ON *rá*, 'a boundary' or *rá*, 'roe deer'. (See p 22.)

A wood on a steep hillside was OE *hangra* or *hongra*. It is found in well-known place-names such as Oakhanger Ha (OE *āc*) and also Clayhanger Ch, D, St, Clehonger He and Clinger Do, Gl. These three last names have OE *clæg*, 'clay', descriptive of the soil on which the woods were situated.

Besides the words OE *lēah* and ON *þveit*, denoting 'a clearing', there was the term *feld*, implying a broader tract that was free of trees, which is best rendered as 'open country'. It is found as the ending of many place-names in formerly wooded country, such as The Weald of the South-East and the southern parts of East Anglia. Its modern equivalent, 'field', probably began to acquire its present meaning of 'an enclosed plot of land' towards the end of the fourteenth century.

A farm (*tūn*) in open country was Felton He, Nb, Sa, So. Hatfield Ess, He, Nt, Wo, YW, and elsewhere, has the same derivation as Heathfield Cu, D, Do, Ha, Sr, Sx, Wo, Wt, YW etc; these places were unwooded and heather-(OE *hǣð*) covered. Maresfield Sx and Marshfield Gl were identical, 'marshy (OE *mersc*) open country'; Bradfield and Broadfield, both common names, have OE *brād*, 'broad' as first element; the Whitefields had light-coloured (*hwīt*, 'white') soil and so on. Chesterfield Db, St were situated in 'open country near or belonging to a fortification (OE *ceaster*)'; Sheffield YW is on the River Sheaf (OE *scǣð*, 'boundary'), but Sheffield Sx was 'open country where sheep (OE *scēap*) grazed'; and there are very many more names ending in -field with a wide variety of descriptive elements.

FRUIT TREES

As a supplement to a diet deficient in greenstuff, fruit in its season was no doubt greatly welcomed; and some kinds could be stored for later use, such as nuts (OE *hnutu*). This word is found in Nutley Ess, Ha, Sx and in Nuthurst La, Sx, Wa—all implying woods or copses—and in Nuthall Wt, which has as its ending OE *h(e)alh*, 'a nook or corner of land'. The hazel is specifically referred to in Haseley Bk, O, Wt and in Heswall Ch, where a spring or stream (OE *wella* in the Mercian form *wælla*) was bordered by them. At Sloley Nf, Wa there were woods of blackthorn or sloe (OE *slāh*); and sloe trees (*slāhtrēow*) are the origin or part-origin of names such as Slaughter(s) and Slaughterford Sx. Slaughterford W is from *slāh-þorn*, literally 'sloe-thorn', but the Gloucestershire (Upper and Lower) Slaughter has a quite different derivation. It is from OE *slōhtre*, 'a mire or slough', and the villages are situated close to a brook with a marshy valley; at least so it was when the settlements were established. It may well be imagined how these names have provided speculative antiquaries with a slaughterous field-day.

Cultivated fruits were hardly known in Saxon England except where trees imported in Roman times had perpetuated themselves by seed or suckers. The plum (OE *plume*) was apparently grown at the many Plumptons and a 'plum-tree wood' or 'plum tree in a clearing' occurred at Plumley Ch. The pear (OE *peru*) gave name to Parham Gl, Sf, Sx and the pear tree (OE *pirige* or *pyrige*) to Perton St, Pirton Hrt, Wo, Pyrton O and Purton Gl, St, W, all of which had 'pear orchards'. The variation of the first vowel in these names between 'e', 'i', 'u' and 'y' illustrates the local developments of OE *ȳ*. Perry Hu, K, St is a development of *pyrige* without a suffix. It will be noticed that *tūn* in these and some later place-names had the meaning 'enclosure' and that they are rendered as 'orchard'.

The many Appletons referred to orchards of apple trees (*æppel*), though Ap(p)ley L, La, Sa, So, Wt probably did not mean 'apple wood', but 'apple tree(s) in a clearing'. However, *æppel* was also used of fruit in general, so that the meaning is far from certain. So too the Applebys of the Danelaw (Db, L, Lei, We) may have been 'fruit farms' rather than simply 'apple farms'. The place-name Appledore D, K is derived from a related word *apuldor* (compare *mapuldor*, p 46); but the Cornish Appledore originally had -*ford* as a suffix and meant 'ford by an apple tree'.

SOME OTHER PLANTS

The water iris, which provided a yellow dye from the blooms and a black pigment from the roots, besides having medicinal and household uses, was a commoner plant than it is today. It was called *lǣfer* in Old English and is found in the name Learmouth Nb, Leverton L and Lever La. The shape of this plant, stylised, gave the heraldic *fleur-de-lys*. The Middle English word *flegge* or *flagge* was applied to the same species and is the origin of Flegg Nf and possibly of Flagg Db. It thrives in much the same damp spots as mint (OE *minte*), which afforded oil for flavouring; and the raw plant could be similarly used. Minstead Ha, Sx (with *stede*, 'a place'), and Minety W (with *ēg*, 'island'), are instances of its occurrence in place-names.

The acrid wild garlic or ramsons (OE *hramsa*, *hramsan* in the plural) is mainly a woodland plant and Romsley Sa, Wo, with the ending *lēah*, suggests as much. Its preference for damp soils is reflected in the ending of Ramsey Ess, Hu (*ēg*). In drier situations, the leek (OE *lēac*) is still native. In early times it was used as food only in times of dearth. The word occurs in Leckhampstead Bk, Brk, combined with *hām-stede*, 'homestead' and Leckhampton Gl, with *hām-tūn*, 'home-farm', but it may have had a secondary meaning, as in the many Leightons and Laughtons, which were probably 'herb gardens'.

The OE word *brēr* was apparently used of any thorny bush and not only of the wild rose. In modern English 'briar' or 'brier' is also ambiguous as a plant-name in that it is used of a heather (French *bruyère*), the roots of which are made into tobacco-pipes, and of the wild rose. Brierley St, YW would have been a clearing in which thorny shrubs grew and Brereton Ch may have been a farm enclosure constructed by planting them. The fruits

52

of one of these plants, the rose, called nowadays either 'hip' or 'hep' (OE *hēopa*) gives us Hetton Du, with *dūn*, 'hill', and, more surprisingly, Shipton YE, YN. In these Yorkshire names there was a change in the early Middle English to the initial 'sh' sound. The same occurred in the change from ON *Hialtland* to the modern form Shetland. Most Shiptons were, of course, 'sheep (OE *scēap*)-farms' (pp 19–20).

Another thorny plant, the bramble (OE *brēmel* etc), an adaptable and very variable shrub with many closely related species, gives name to Bramshaw Ha (*sceaga*) and Bromley Lo (*lēah*). Most instances of Bromley, however, refer to the broom (OE *brōm*), of which the word *brēmel* is a derivative; and *brōm* itself had a wider connotation, like *brēr*, of 'a thorny bush', a meaning found in other Germanic languages. The word *brōm* occurs in scores of place-names, of which some of the more common are Bramley (*lēah*), Brampton and Brompton (*tūn*), all of frequent occurrence; Brandon Du, Nf, Sf, Wa (*dūn*), Bro(o)mfield Cu, Ess, K, So (*feld*), Bromwich St, Wa, (with *wīc*, 'dwelling'), and Bro(o)m(e) Du, K, Nf, Sa, Sf, Wo. The related plant, furze (OE *fyrs*), gives Furze Co, D and Farsley YW; and gorse (OE *gorst*), now applied to the same group of related species, gives Gorsley He, Gl. Whin, another modern alternative name, is derived from ON *hvin* and occurs in names such as Whinfell Cu, We, combined with ON *fjall*, 'mountain', and Winnow Cu, with ON *haugr*, 'hill, cairn'. All of these plants had their uses: the broom in broom-making and in medicine, and gorse in providing kindling when dry or fodder from the young shoots when crushed.

Useful, too, was flax (OE *līn*, ON *lín*), which was grown in arable plots (OE *æcer*) at Linacre(s) C, La, Nb and Lenacre K. Linley Sa (*lēah*), and Linthwaite YW (ON *þveit*) were clearings and Linton C, Db (*tūn*) and Lyneham O, W (*hām*) were farms devoted to its cultivation. The species of flax grown in England before the Middle Ages were the narrow-leaved (*Linum bienne*) and perennial (*L anglicum*), both of limited use in affording fibres for the production of linen. It will be noticed that the OE and ON words and the Latin word for flax have the first syllable in common. The word 'linen' (OE *līnen*) was originally an adjective, 'made of flax'. Flax (OE *fleax*) seems to have been an alternative word for the same plants and is found in similar place-name compounds: Flaxley Gl, YW (*lēah*) and Flaxton (*tūn*). There have been a number of reports of the discovery of this material in Anglo-Saxon graves. At Finglesham, K a woman had been buried in a dress or coverlet of 'linen diamond twill' and fragments of linen were found in the princely cenotaph at Sutton Hoo, Sf. Traces of linen occurred on a Jutish pin from Dover of about AD 600; and there may have been a scrap on a Saxon buckle found with a burial at Horndean Ha. Woollen fabrics have also been found in similar circumstances.

The commonest of our native ferns, the bracken (OE *brǣcen*), explains the name Bracken YE and Brackenthwaite Cu, YW (ON *þveit*). A related form, *bracu* is the source of the place-names Brackley Nth and Braxted Ess (OE *stede*, 'a place'). And it was surely the same plant, called *fearn*, 'fern', that is referred to in Farnham Bk, K, YW (with *hām*, 'homestead'), Farnham Sr (with *hām* or *hamm*, 'enclosure'), Fareham Ha (*hām*). Far(r)ington Brk, Do and Farndon Ch, Nt, all with *dūn*, 'hill', Farnborough Brk, K, with *beorg*, 'hill', Farndale YN (OE *dæl*, Far(n)ley St, YW, Farleigh Ha, K, So, Sr, W, Fairlight Sx and Fairley Sa, all with *lēah*, and very many more. Bracken was burned to provide alkaline ash for soap-making and glass-making and it is still, in some parts of the country, used for bedding in cattle sheds.

There is no single English species of plant that covers such vast areas as heather or ling, whether it be on northern grouse moors, the commons of the south, or heaths in any region. In Saxon times the forests of various kinds were probably even more extensive, but most were situated on cultivable tracts and have for long been felled; the heathlands with their acid soils, poor in mineral salts, have had little economic value except as sparse grazing for sheep or cattle. Some heaths have also provided fuel in the form of peaty turves, and some use has been made of the plants as cattle-bedding and in broom-making.

Moreover, the coarse fibres from heather-stems were used in humble buildings, sometimes even as short-lived thatch. Yet it remains true that the English heathlands have always been largely useless. Only now, with the sprawl of urban areas, are they appreciated as open spaces.

The word heath (OE *hǣð*) gives rise to many names such as the numerous Hatfields (OE *feld*, 'open country'), Headleys (*lēah*, 'clearing'), Hattons ('farm (*tūn*) on a heath'), and the name Heath itself. The midland and northern Hatfields (eg Nt, YE, YW) probably contain ON *heiðr* and in the South-East *hāð*, a form related to *hǣð*, is found in names such as Hoathly K, Sx, Hothfield K and, uncompounded, in Hoad(s) K, Sx. Another word, doubtfully related to *hǣð* is *hǣddre*, the source of our word 'heather', which occurs in Hethersett Nf, with *sǣte*, 'settlers' and in Uttoxeter St prefixed by the personal name *Wuttuc*. The modern word 'ling', an alternative for 'heather' goes back to OE *lyng* and is exemplified in place-names such as Ling L, Nf and Lingwood Nt.

One further common plant-name, 'moss' (OE *mos*, ON *mosi*), which could mean also 'lichen' and 'bog, swamp', is the source of the first element of Moston Ch, La, Sa and of Moseley YW. OE *mēos*, a related word with the same range of meanings gives Meesden Hrt (*dūn*), Mos(e)ley Bk, Nt and, uncompounded, Meece St. Moseley St was '*Moll*'s *lēah*' and Moseley Wo was a '*lēah* infested by mice (OE *mūs*, plural *mȳs*)' or possibly '*Mūs(a)*'s or *Músi*'s *lēah*'.

THE SCRUBLANDS

Where fens and marshes were silting up and where cultivated areas had been abandoned, scrub took over as an intermediate stage before the high forest could become established. The change from marsh to forest was slow, that of former arable fields more rapid. After the departure of the Roman legions at the beginning of the fifth century, the demand for corn dropped greatly, following a slower decline in the later decades of the fourth century. And with chaos in the western provinces of the Empire, trade was disrupted and markets alternative to the Roman army were few. Much land therefore went out of cultivation in Britain and it gradually reverted to something like its primeval state.

The Saxon settlers occupied areas in process of reversion and they had several words to describe the brushwood or scrub that they found. Heston Mx (*tūn*), Heysham La (*hām*) and Hayes K, Mx, Wo contain the word *hǣs*; Truscott Co (with *cot(e)*, 'cottage') and Trusley Db (*lēah*) have *trūs* as their first element; and Ris(e)ley Bd, Brk, Db, K, La and Ruston Nf contain the words *hrīs*. OE *scrubb*, the source of our words 'scrub' and 'shrub', also meaning 'brushwood', is the origin of the many Shrub(s) Farms; and OE *snār*, giving Snow (Hill) Lo, Sr and possibly Snoreham Ess (*hām*), as well as *spearca*, which occurs in Sparkford Ha, So —have a similar connotation. The majority of these names originally ending in -*cot*, -*hām* or *tūn* indicate settlement in the areas of brushwood, for they were easier to clear and cultivate than the virgin forest. And the names ending in -*lēah*, meaning 'clearing' in this context, suggest fields that had been carved out of the forest and which had been reinvaded by scrub after their abandonment by the Romano–Britons.

The word *hrīs* occurs a number of times in conjunction with the word *brycg*, 'bridge', as in Ricebridge Sx, Ridgebridge Sr, Roy's Bridge Nt, where 'bridge' possibly refers to a causeway constructed of brushwood across a marsh. If this were so, the building material was probably near at hand growing in the wet soil. At a later date, the ON word *kjarr* was used of brushwood growing on marsh. This term is exemplified in place-names such as Redcar YN, compounded with OE *hrēod*, 'reed', and in Broadcarr Nf (OE *brād*, 'broad'), which is self-explanatory.

CHAPTER 4

Rivers, Lakes, Ponds and Marshes

Places had names even before the English came to Britain, but not many of them survived in use after the Saxon conquest. Most pre-English names were probably given by people who spoke a Celtic language and the names surviving can sometimes be seen to have a close relationship with Old Welsh or Old Irish words. The commonest survivals are river-names and they exist in most counties.

Some of these Celtic names, such as Avon W—Ha, W—Gl, Wa—Gl, meant simply 'river'; the Axe So, the Exe So—D, the Esk, Cu, YN, all derive from the Celtic word *iscā* (Old Irish *esc*), which had the meaning 'water'. The river-name Derwent Cu, Db, Nb, YE goes back to a Celtic word for 'oak', as do the originally identical names Darent K, Dart D and Darwen La. But a number of major rivers have names that are inexplicable. The Thames, the Thame O, the Tame St—Wa, La—YW, YN, the Team Du, the Teme Sa—Wo, the Tavy D and the Tamar Co, D all go back to the same Celtic root which is represented in modern Welsh place-names by the rivers Taff and Taf. Another enigmatic group is the Colne Ess, Hrt—Mx—Bk, La, YW and the Clun Sa, Nt. The Gloucestershire Coln is shown by its earliest recorded spellings to have had an origin different from that of the Colnes, but its meaning is also unknown.

The Lune We—La, the Teign D, the Tees Du, YN, the Severn Sa—Wo—Gl, the Tyne Nb, Du and many more rivers great and small are of doubtful meaning or quite inexplicable.

From these rivers, many towns and villages took their names.

Exeter was 'the fort or fortified town (OE *ceaster*) on the Exe'; Colchester and Lancaster, with endings more obviously derived from *ceaster*, are on the Colne and Lune. Names such as Exmouth, Avonmouth, Teignmouth, Tynemouth and Dartmouth have OE *mūða*, 'an estuary' as their termination. The towns Darwen La, Thame O and the villages Clun Nt, Sa, Clowne Db and Colne Ess are named from the rivers on which they stand. Indeed, no small proportion of our village and town names were formerly river-names, either wholly or in part.

But there are some Celtic river-names which are of more than usual interest. For instance, the Old British word *cambo-*, 'crooked', may survive in the names of the rivers Cam Gl and Camel Co, as well as in Cambeck Cu ('crooked beck' [ON *bekkr*]); but it is difficult to distinguish this British word from OE *camb* and ON *kambr*, meaning 'a comb or crest of a ridge', which more certainly occur in place-names such as Cambs YN, (The) Combs Cu, Db, Sf, Cambs Head YN and Cambridge St, the last of these having OE *hrycg*, 'a ridge' as its ending. It is worthy of note, too, that the more famous River Cam takes its name by back-formation from Cambridge; and that the Somerset places, Queen and West Camel, derive their names from another Old British word, *canto-*, 'edge, border', which also gave rise to the names Kent and Quantock So. Queen Camel is so called because it was in the possession of Eleanor, the wife of Edward I, and West Camel is to the west of the Queen's manor.

The process of back-formation, mentioned in connection with the Cam and Cambridge, began even in Saxon times. If the first part of a town-name had ceased to have meaning, it might, especially if it were compounded with -bridge or -ford, be thought to represent the name of a river. Chelmsford Ess, for instance, was *Cēolmǣr*'s ford. By the early thirteenth century it had become *Chel(e)mer(e)ford*, with a variety of spellings, and the Saxon personal name was long forgotten. It was then assumed, quite unconsciously, that the town-name meant 'ford over the Chelmer' and by the later sixteenth century, at least, the river was being referred to by that name. Some back-formations, such as the naming of the River Adur Sx from the supposition that the Roman harbour of *Portus Adurni* had been at its estuary, are quite late. In this instance, the poet Drayton was responsible, in his 'Polyolbion' of 1612. Other examples of the process are Pang, from Pangbourne Brk, 'stream (OE *burna*) of *Pāga*'s people', which was, in fact, the name of the stream before it became attached to the settlement; the Chor from Chorley La, '*lēah* of the peasants (*ceorl*)'; and the Wandle from Wandsworth Sr (p 78).

Another British word for 'crooked', *crumbo-*, gives Crummock (Water), though this Cumbrian lake is no more irregular than most; and from the same word are derived the Croome villages of Worcestershire, which are situated along a winding (crooked) stream. There was also an OE *crumb*, 'crooked', obviously, but obscurely related to *crumbo-*. The English word is contained in the first syllables of Cromford Db and Cromwell Nt, YW, the latter ending in OE *wella*, which must have meant 'stream' in this compound. A related OE noun *crumbe*, 'a bend', occurs in Crompton La, which would have meant 'farm (*tūn*) in the bend (of a river)'. Some other OE and ON words for 'crooked' are noted in a later paragraph.

Other pre-English words that were applied to rivers are *dacrū*, probably meaning 'water', in Dacre YW and Dacre Beck Cu; an adjective *dubo-*, 'black', in Dawlish D and Douglas La, both having as second element the British word *glassjo-*, 'stream'; and *dubo-* alone as Dove Db, YN, YW. The distinct British word *dubro-*, 'water', occurring in modern names as Dore He, Dover K and, as a second element in Andover, Micheldever and Candover Ha, was also combined with the Celtic *caled* to give names such as Calder Cu, La, YW and Cawder (Gill) YW. These meant 'rocky (*caled*) stream (*dubro-*)'. Moreover, the British word for an elm tree, *lemo-*, is the origin of the place-names Lymn L, Lympne K and of the river-name Leam Wa, on which stand Leamington Spa and Leamington Hastings, 'farms on the River Leam'. The addition 'Hastings' commemorates a late thirteenth-century holder of the manor.

A final instance of a British word surviving in a modern river-name is *Trisantonā*, of which the meaning is unknown. The Devon Trent and the great Midland river of that name, besides the Tarrant streams, Do, R are derived from this word. The old name of the Arun Sx was Tarrant; its present name is a back-formation from Arundel, which was 'a valley (OE *dell*) where the plant called hore-hound (OE *hārhūne*) grew'.

We have already had instances of names compounded with OE *burna*, 'stream'. In its simple form it appears now as Bourn(e) C, Ha, Li; Burnham Li was originally the dative plural *burnum*, 'at the streams', but Burnham Bk, Ess, Nf is a compound with *hām*, 'homestead by a stream' and the common name Sherbo(u)rne was 'a clear (OE *scīr*) stream'. Compounds with -bourne are very common, but in the Danelaw they may be derived from the cognate ON *brunnr*, 'well, spring' or the Old Norse may have replaced the similar Old English word.

Although it came into use in place-names somewhat later than *burna*, OE *brōc*, 'brook, stream' is equally common and as widespread. It gives Brook(e), a frequently-recurring minor name, as well as numerous compounds such as Brocton St, Brockton Sa and Broughton Bk, Cu, Db, Hu, La, Lei, Nt, O, W, Wa, Wo, YN, YW, all meaning 'farm by a stream'. But several Broughtons (the one near Manchester, three in Shropshire and one each in Li, Nth, St, Sx) have the same origin as the very common name Burton, which is from OE *burh-tūn*, 'farm in or near a fort'. Yet a third derivation for Broughton was from OE *beorg-tūn*, 'farm near a hill or barrow, or on a hill'. The names with this origin are in Lincolnshire, near Brigg and in Hampshire. Of the many other compounds with *brōc*, the commonest is Brockley Lo, Sf, So, though the London and Somerset instances may have been '*Brōca*'s *lēah* and a third possibility is an origin in *brocc*, 'a badger' (see p 24). Millbrook Bd, Ha refers to a stream which worked a mill (OE *mylen*).

A word long lost from our vocabulary but entering into many place-names, is OE *ēa*, 'river, stream'. It is cognate with Latin *aqua*, which is most closely paralleled in the Germanic languages by Gothic *ahwa*. The Latin word is the origin of French *eau*, with which *ēa* (Middle English *ee*) was sometimes confused in documents and this confusion accounts for the spelling Eau L and (South) Eau C. Other modern forms from *ēa* are Eye (Brook) La and also Rea C, Sa, Wa, Wo and Ray Bk, O. The prefixed 'r' in these two latter forms arose from the phrase 'at the stream', which was OE *æt þǣre ēa*, becoming in Middle English *atter ee*, and then, through misunderstanding of the extinct word *ee*, *atte ree*, with the 'r' wrongly attached to the final word. The surname Attree has the same origin. In the South-West the river-names Yeo, So, D have developed by a process almost peculiar to the local dialects. Elsewhere, the commonest compound is Eaton, 'farm by the stream', found in nine counties. The more famous Eton Bk was formerly identical with these.

Several Old English river-names were onomatopoeic, that is, the pronunciation of the Old English name roughly echoed the sound of the water. Lymm Ch is from OE *hlimme*, 'the resounding one' and the rivers Lyn(n) D, Wt, meaning 'torrent', are derived from OE *hlynn*, 'the noisy one'. Lydbrook Gl, Liddel (Water) Cu, with OE *dæl*, 'dale', and the rivers Lyd(e) D, He, So are from OE *hlȳde*, 'the loud one'; indeed, this OE word is a mutated form of *hlūd*, the source of our adjective 'loud'. This OE word, too, gives rise to place-names such as Louth L, named from the River Lud; and there are numerous instances of *hlūd* in combination with *wella*, 'spring, stream', such as Ludwell Db, Nth, So and Ludhill YE, YW. Ludbrooke D and Ludford Sa also imply 'sounding water', but in Loudham Nt, Sf and Luddesdown K we have the personal name *Hlūda*, 'the loud man'. The name of the River Loud La is from the related noun, OE *hlūde*.

The Danes had a similar concept in the naming of streams. The River Skell YW and Skelwith La have ON *skjallr*, 'resounding', as first element. The second element of Skelwith was ON *vað*, 'a ford', but the resounding noise was presumably from a nearby waterfall rather than from the ford. Another ON word for 'brook' was *lǽkr* or *lákr*, an alternative to *bekkr*, of which we have already had several examples. It occurs as Leake L, Nt, YN and Leek St, Wa. The related OE *lacu* is also fairly common, as in Kerslake Co (cress [OE *cerse*], -'stream'), Shiplake O (*scēap*, 'sheep') and the River Medlock La, which meant 'meadow (OE *mǣd*)-stream'. And another related word, OE *lǣcc*, 'stream, bog', gives the name of the River Leach Gl, from which we have Eastleach, Northleach, and Lechlade. The fairly common Latchmoor or Latchmore D, Ess, Ha, Sr, W and Latchmere Sr, all containing *mere*, 'a pool', may have either the above-mentioned *lǣcc* or *lǣce*, 'a leech', the creature formerly used in medicine for drawing off human blood (p 32).

Two other OE words for 'stream or brook' are *riđ*, which gives Ryde Sr, Wt, Shepreth C ('sheep-stream'), and Tingrith Bd, which was a stream beside which an assembly (OE, ON *þing*) was wont to meet; and *sīc* from which Sykes YW and many field-names bordering streams are derived (eg Syke C). In the Dane-law ON *sík*, 'ditch or trench', may occur instead of or replacing OE *sīc*. (See pp 67–8 for OE *wella* and its variants.)

The confluence of two streams is represented by several words. OE *twisla* is the source of Twisel(l) Nb, Twisleton YW (*tūn*), of Entwisle La (either a personal name *Enna* or *ened*, 'a duck'), Oswaldtwistle (*Ōswald*) and Haltwhistle Nb (with Old French *haut*, 'high'). The same idea is expressed by OE *ēa-mōt*, 'waters' meet' in Eamont Cu and Emmetts La and by the cognate ON *á-mót* in Aymot YN. The idea of confluence is also conveyed by OE (*ge-*) *mỹđe*, which is a mutated form of *mūđa*, '(river-)mouth' (p 58). Mitford Nb, Mitton La, Wo, YE, YN (*tūn*) and Mytholmroyd YW are derived from this word. The West Riding place-name has it with the dative plural in -um and the suffix *rodu*, meaning as a whole 'clearing at the confluence(s)'.

The course of a river may be interrupted by a waterfall, which in Old Norse was *fors*. Fossdale YN and High Force Du, YN are derived from it. OE *wætergefall* meant not only 'waterfall' as in Waterfall YN and Watervale D, but 'swallow-hole', as in Waterfall St, where a stream goes underground. A deep place in a river, or a whirlpool was *wēl* in Old English. Thelwall Ch was such a place crossed by a plank (OE *þel*) bridge. The curious Lancashire name Sale Wheel has *salh*, 'willow' as the word qualifying *wēl*, and the whole name presumably meant 'a river-pool bordered by willows'.

A wide variety of epithets is applied to rivers in order to distinguish one from another. The Old Welsh *winn* (modern Welsh *gwyn*) is coupled with Celtic *dubro-* (Welsh *dwfr*) in the name Wendover Bk, 'the white (chalky) water or stream' (see p 59). Another meaning of *winn* occurs in Wenlock Sa, which meant 'holy monastery' (old Welsh *loc*). It is possible that Wendover originally referred to a 'holy stream' or it was equivalent in meaning to English names such as the common Whitwell, from OE *hwīt*, 'white', or Whitburn Du, from ON *hvitr*, its cognate. Sherborne (p 60) has OE *scīr*, 'clear' and Smite (Brook) Lei, Nt, Wa, Wo has the opposite meaning of 'dirty' (OE *smīte*). Freshwater Wt implies estuarial water that was not brackish and Friskney L means the same, with OE *fresc*, 'fresh' and *ēa*, 'water'. Saltburn YN and Saltmarsh(e) Gl, He, Sx, YE require no explanation.

A cool (OE *cōl*) stream or spring is referred to in Colburn YN and Colwell Nb, Wt and a cold (OE *cald*) one by Chadwell Ess and Caldbeck Cu (ON *kaldr* and ON *bekkr*). The noun, OE *celde*, related to *cōl* and *cald*, is found in Bapchild and Honeychild K with the personal names *Bacca* and *Hūna*; and in Learchild Nb with the personal name *Lēofrīc*.

Apart from OE *crumb*, 'crooked', mentioned above, and OE *wōh*, 'crooked', the origin of the first element in Wo(o)burn Bd, Bk, Sr, there was the OE noun *hōc*, 'a bend in a river', in the common name Hook(e) and OE *horn*(*a*), with the same meaning, in Horncastle L and Horley O—all implying the meandering of streams. The ON noun *krókr*, 'a bend' occurs in Crook(s) Du, La, We, Nb, YW and in northern field-names, where it is applied to land in the bend of a river.

River-crossings of various kinds are to be expected in the names of places, for settlements commonly grew up beside them to give harbourage to travellers and to benefit from the trade they brought. Many places with names in -ford (OE *ford*) have become important for this reason. Bedford (*Bēda*'s), Bradford (*brād*, 'broad'), Retford (*rēad*, 'red'), Stafford (*stæð*, 'shore'), and many more, are now major towns. The Welsh *rhyd*, with the same meaning, survives in English place-names in those regions where Celtic speech survived longest, as in Redmain Cu (with Welsh *maen*, 'a stone') and Penrith Cu (with British *pen(n)*, 'head or chief'); and alone in Rhydd Wo. Another synonym, OE (*ge-*) *wæd* (related to the verb 'to wade' and to Latin *vādere*, 'to go' and *vadum*, 'a ford'), is represented by such names as Wadebridge Co, where the bridge (OE *brycg*) superseded a ford, as also at both East and West Bridgford Nt; by Landwade C, 'a long (OE *lang*) ford'; by Biggleswade Bd, originally controlled by a man named *Biccel*; and by the simplex Wade Sf. The cognate ON *vað* gives Wath Cu, YN, YW and Sandwith Cu, YW which has the same meaning as the many Sandfords and Sampfords (OE *sand*).

Another word, OE (*ge-*)*lād*, meant 'passage over a river' and occurs uncompounded in Load So and Lode C, Gl. The Gloucestershire name Framilode indicates a passage across the Severn at the confluence with the tributary River Frome (Old British *frām*, 'fair, brisk'); and Lechlade Gl is at the meeting of the rivers Leach and Thames. In this name we may, however, have another meaning of (*ge-*)*lād*, namely 'watercourse' (of the River Leach). It is interesting to note that the medial 'i' of Framilode is a vestige of the *ge-* of *ge-lād*. In some instances of its use at a later period this word seems to have acquired the meaning 'ferry', especially along the Severn in Gloucestershire where ferries came to operate from the several places with names ending in -lode. Besides Framilode, there are Lower and Upper Lode, Wainlode ('wagon [OE *wægn*] river-crossing'), Abloads (*Abba*'s), and St Mary de Lode in the city of Gloucester. But the word ferry itself is derived from ON *ferja*, a word related to OE *ferian*, 'to carry' and it did not come into general use until the end of the Middle Ages. The ON word is found in North and

South Ferriby, which were settlements (ON *bý*) at each end of a ferry across the Humber. It had existed in prehistoric times, for a very ancient boat was found at each of these places; and a little upstream there was a Roman ferry.

Where rivers were unnavigable for a short stretch, it is likely that a portage had to be made. This is probably indicated by the use of the OE word *dræg*, which is related to the verb *dragan*, 'to drag or draw'. Drayton Ha, L, Mx, Nt meant 'farm by a place of portage', but most other Draytons, and there are many, probably refer to a farm near a track along which timber or other heavy goods were dragged. The topography of these places makes it unlikely that they were named from a portage. Draycot(t) or -cote was a shed (OE *cot*) where drays or sleds were housed.

ISLANDS

An island (*ēg*) in a river or in marshland gave name to many places. Eyam Db is the dative plural, ending in -*um*, of this word. Sandy Bd has it as a final element as has Whitney He, in which we have the dative singular, *hwītan*, of the adjective *hwīt*, 'white', the name originally meaning 'at the white island'. Thorney C, Mx, So, Sx was an *ēg* on which grew thorn trees (*þorn*); Goosey Bk was characterised by geese (*gōs*), Horsey Nf, So by horses (*hors*) and Sheppey K by sheep (*scēap*). Witney O contains the personal name *Witta* and Aldersey Ch has the personal name *Aldhere* or *Æþelric*. The cognate ON *ey* is found in the name Lundy (Island) combined with ON *lundi*, 'a puffin' and in Walney La, which must have been a patch of firm land surrounded by quagmire (OE *wagen*). Nayland Sf was originally *ēg-land*, which, prefixed by *atten* in the Middle Ages ('at the island') acquired its present form by erroneous separation of the 'n' from *atten* and its attachment to the following word (*cp* p 61). The reverse process has happened with the OE word *næddre*, whereby 'a nadder' has become 'an adder'. In Ryland C a misdivision similar to that of Nayland has occurred, this time with *atter*, 'at the', which normally would have preceded a feminine noun. Though *ēg* was feminine, *ēg-land* had the gender of its second element, which was neuter. It is not surprising, however, that medieval peasants had little care for the niceties of Middle English grammar. Another derivative of *ēg*, namely *ēgeð*, 'a small island', gives rise to the names of islets in the rivers Thames and Severn, such as (Brentford and Isleworth) Aits or Neight Wo. The latter has an attached 'n' as in Nayland.

The Primitive Welsh *inis*, 'island', occurs as Ince Ch, La and, combined with OE *cȳpe*, 'an osier basket' (for the catching of fish), gives Inskip La. Far commoner, however, is the ON word *holmr*, 'isle or water-meadow', which is represented by the common place-name Holme and by compounds such as Durham, in which the first element was OE *dūn*, 'hill', and the second ON *holmr*. The sea-girt islands of Flat Holme and Steep Holme in the Bristol Channel may have OE *holm*, 'the sea', but this term was probably confused with *holmr* in late Old English and the confusion would have been the easier in these instances because the islands were used as bases by the Vikings when raiding the adjacent coasts. They were starved out of one or other of these islands in AD 917, but the manuscripts of the *Anglo-Saxon Chronicle* which record the event disagree as to which island it was. Flat Holme was the island of the fleet (ON *floti*), but its silhouette, as seen from the Somerset coast, is indeed 'flat' as compared with the neighbouring Steep (OE *stēap*) Holme.

The Old Danish cognate *hulm*, with the same meanings, is found less often, as in Hulme Ch, La, St, Levenshulme La (with the woman's name *Lēofwine*) and Oldham La, which was 'the old (OE *ald*) island or water-meadow'.

Of the other islands round our coasts, the Scillies have a pre-English name of unknown meaning. Wight, however, is mentioned by classical writers as *Vectis*, which may be a Celtic word cognate with Latin *vectis*, 'a lever' and with our word 'weight' (OE *wiht*) and the meaning is assumed to be 'that which rises above the sea, an island'. It has been suggested that the name Thanet K is of Celtic origin, too. If it indeed meant 'fire-island', the reference was probably to a Roman lighthouse marking the channel which led to the Roman fort at Richborough.

Of islands with English names, Canvey Ess was 'the island of *Cana*'s people (*Caninga*)', and Foulness Ess was 'the wild birds' (*fugol*) headland (*næss*). Far to the north, the Farne Islands Nb were probably so called because they were overgrown with bracken-fern (*fearn*), and Holy Island Nb because of its association with early Northumbrian monasticism. The alternative name, Lindisfarne, was in use at least as early as the third decade of the eighth century. It appears to mean 'the island of the people who go to Lindsey' (p 70) or 'the island of the Lindsey people'.

SPRINGS

The sources of rivers were of major interest to the early inhabitants of England in affording uncontaminated supplies of water for men and domestic animals. They took over the word *funtōn* in the form *funta* from the conquered Britons and in the South they used the term in not a few place-names. Bedfont Mx and Bedmond Hrt, originally identical, had springs fed into tubs (*byden*) to provide a sufficient depth of water to make its drawing easy; or, less likely, the springs broke surface in hollows of the shape of a tub. Bedwell Hrt and Bidwell Bd, D, Nth have the same first element, but it is combined with the normal Old English word for a spring, namely *wella*. Boarhunt Ha was a spring near a fort (*burh*) and Mottisfont Ha was one near a meeting-place (*mōt*). In Chalfont Bk we have the personal name *Ceadel* and in Havant Ha, the name *Hāma*. A later loan-word, Old French *fontein*, with the same meaning, and obviously cognate with the Celtic word, gives Fountains (Abbey) YW.

The more usual word for 'a spring', OE *wella*, has already been mentioned several times in earlier pages. Apart from names such as Well Ha, K, L, YN and Wells Nf, So, we have Bradwell Bk, Ess, Sf or Broadwell Gl, Sx referring to width; Stanwell Mx and

Stowell Gl, So, W describing its lining of stone (*stān*); and scores more names in -well. OE *ǣwell* had a similar meaning, 'spring or stream'. It was originally a compound of *ēa*, 'water', and *wella*. Alton Do, Ha, Ewell K, Sr and Carshalton Sr, 'cress (*cærse*)— spring-farm (*tūn*)', are derived from it; and *ǣwelm*, a similar compound of *ēa* and of *welm*, 'spring', accounts for Ewelme O and Ewen Gl.

The modern noun 'spring' (OE *spring*) has a variety of meanings, some of them unknown to the Anglo-Saxons. The sense 'source of a stream' occurs early, but place-names given in medieval times and containing this term may refer to 'a small branch (of a plant), a young plantation or a copse'. Springthorpe L, which is mentioned in the Domesday Book of 1086, probably meant 'farm or hamlet by a river-spring', but Springfield, which is common as a minor name, may refer to a copse or, if it is late name in origin, to a field ploughed or grazed in the spring of the year. The use of the word 'spring' as a season is not found in literature before 1530, although it was probably in spoken use long before that time.

POOLS, PONDS AND LAKES

As with so many other categories of words, those referring to sheets of water were more numerous in Old English than they are in modern usage. Perhaps the commonest in place-names is OE *mere*, 'a pool or the sea'. Mere Ch, L and Meare So are developments of the word uncompounded and referred to freshwater pools. Combined with *tūn*, 'a farm', are Martin Ha, K, La, L, Nt, Wo; Marton Ch, La, L, Sa, Wa, We, YE, YN, YW and Merton D, Nf, O. Grasmere We is still a 'grass (*gærs*)-lake', but many of these stretches of water have long since been drained away. In Margate K we have this same word used of the sea, the 'gate' referring to a gap in the cliffs; in Mersea Ess the second element is *ēg*, 'island' as is made clear in one of the manuscripts of the *Anglo-Saxon Chronicle* which refers to the place as 'an island out at sea called Mersea'.

Modern English 'sea' is derived from OE *sǣ* which, like *mere*, could mean both 'lake' or 'sea'. It refers to the latter in Seaton Cu, Du, D, Nb, which were 'farms by the sea'; but in Seaton YE it must have been an inland stretch of water, perhaps a vaster Hornsea Mere, near which the settlement of Seaton was established. Seathwaite La was a clearing (ON *þveit*) beside Seathwaite Tarn. And in place-names such as Derwent Water we have OE *wæter* used of a lake, in this instance characterised by the river that flows through it. Semerwater YN is a strange tautological compound of *sǣ*, *mere* and *wæter*. It began as OE *sǣ* (or perhaps as ON *sǽr*) and the other elements were added successively. Semer Sf and Seamer YN are half-way through the same process, with *mere* added to *sǣ* after the latter word had lost the meaning 'lake'; and *wæter* also was added to the North Riding name.

A pool or pond (and sometimes a creek) could be referred to as *pōl* or *pull*, as in Pool(e) Ch, D, Do, Gl, YW or Poulton, a frequent place-name. Liverpool and Blackpool La were places named from the colour of the water in the pools beside which the settlements grew up. The relationship of this word to Welsh *pwll* and ON *pollr* is not clear, but OE *pyll*, 'a tidal creek, or pool in a river' is a mutated form of *pull*. It occurs mainly in Somerset names such as Pilton, Huntspill (with the personal name *Hūn*) and Uphill, which should be compared with several river-names prefixed with OE *upp-*, for example Upavon, W and Upottery D, which are further 'up' stream than Netheravon (ie the 'lower') and than Otterton and Ottery St Mary. Uphill So, however, was 'up' in the sense 'above', for it is on higher ground, though near the estuary of the Axe. Mention should also be made of another derivative of *pōl* or *pull*, namely *polra*, 'marshy land', as in Powderham D (with *hām*, 'homestead'); in Pollard YE and Poulders K, both originally *polra* without addition. The cognate 'polder' of the Low Countries was a later borrowing into English.

An older word for 'pool' is the pre-English *lindo-* (Welsh *llyn*), which formed the first syllable of Lincoln; the second is from Latin *colōnia*, 'a colony', for the city was founded as a place of permanent settlement for time-expired veterans of the Roman Ninth Legion who had long known it as the fortress they had garrisoned. Lindsey, the region adjacent to the north of the city, probably took its name from the same pool, and Lindisfarne (p 67) in turn acquired its name from Lindsey. This region was perhaps named from an island (*ēg*) in the marshes of the River Witham, near a pool in that river. In fact, Witham is also a Celtic name, perhaps in its first element related to the Welsh word *gwydd* which, as a noun, means 'goose' or 'trees' (though with different inflected forms); or as an adjective it means 'wild, uncultivated', an apt description of marshes. The Norfolk name (King's) Lynn may go back to the same Celtic word *lindo-*, referring to a pool near the mouth of the River Ouse.

There are several other words that were applied to small areas of water. OE *lum(m)*, 'a pool', is the first syllable of Lumley Du, of Lumford Db and of Lomax La. The first two of these names have the endings *lēah*, 'a wood' and *ford*, but the third was *halh*, 'a corner of land', if one takes the usual meaning, but here, perhaps, it may have been 'a water-meadow'. Lumb La, YW is a modern form of the word uncompounded. And OE *dympel* had the meaning of 'a pool in a wood or a dell', surviving in the names Dimple(s) La, YW and Dumplington La. The last of these is an *-ingtūn* compound with some such meaning as 'farm by the pool in the wood or in the dell'. ON *dembil*, 'a pool' gives Dembleby L (with ON *bý*, 'farm') and OE *dubb*, 'a pool' is represented by Dub (Beck) Cu and (St Ellen) Dubb La.

Onomatopoeia must be the origin of OE *plæsc*, 'a pool' in Plashford Co, Melplash Do (with OE *myln*, 'a mill') and Pla(i)sh Sa, So; and the same is true of the Old Danish *flask*, which is the source of many minor names like Flash L, Nt, St. The common word 'puddle' (OE *puddel*) is found only in later place-names such as Puddle (Dock) Lo, Ess, Sx; and 'pond' (ME *ponde*), which is widespread in modern usage, does not appear in records before about 1300 or in any but minor place-names.

The ON word for 'lake', *vatn*, which is related to 'water', occurs in the place-names Wasdale We, compounded with ON *dalr*, 'dale' and in Watendlath Cu, which seems to have meant 'hill (OE *hlāw*) at the end (ON *endi*) of the lake'. This sheet of water is nowadays called a 'tarn', from ON *tjǫrn*, 'a small lake'. Of numerous instances of its use in the northern counties, one may cite Blea Tarn Cu, which has the ON adjective *blár*, 'dark'; and Malham Tarn YW with what seems to have been the dative plural (in *-um*) of a rare ON word *malgi* or *malh*, 'a bag', probably used in a topographical sense with an extension of meaning to 'bag-like hollow'.

SEA INLETS

One of the commoner words for an indentation of the coastline was OE *flēot*, 'an estuary or inlet'. It occurs without a qualifying epithet as Fleet Do, Ha, K, L, Mx, though the inland instances must have had the alternative meaning of 'river', as had the cognate ON *fljót*. The German verb 'fliessen', 'to flow' and the modern English 'float' are also cognates. Benfleet Ess was a 'tree-marked creek' or one that could be crossed by a 'beam' (OE *bēam*) of timber, serving as a bridge; Swinefleet YW is tautological if the first element was OE *swin*, 'a creek or a channel' rather than OE *swīn*, 'swine, pigs'.

A cove (OE *cofa*) was originally 'an inner chamber' or 'a cave'. The latter word, by the way, is not related to 'cove', directly at any rate, but is a borrowing via French of the Latin *cava*, 'hollows'. By an extension in meaning, *cofa* came to mean 'a sea inlet' by the sixteenth century. In some place-names, as for example Cobham Sr, Covenham L (both with *hām*) and Coventry Wa (with *trēow*, 'tree') the personal name *Cofa* occurs, but in Covehurst (Bay) Sx and in Cove D, Ha, Sf we may have the modern sense of 'cove'. The word 'bay', from Old French *baie*, is found only in medieval and modern place-names and not at all in Old English.

The rare place-name element ON *vík*, 'creek, bay' is found in a few northern names such as Runswick (Bay), with a personal name, and in Wigtoft L, in which it is combined with ON *topt*, 'the plot of ground on which a dwelling stands'.

ARTIFICIAL CHANNELS

As the regions of earliest occupation became over-populated, new colonies had to be established in virgin territory, much of which was either forest, on medium or heavy soils, or undrained areas in the river valleys or on the margins of fens. Dwelling-sites could be found on higher patches of gravel in the marshes, but crops could only be grown in soil that was not saturated for much of the year. A system of drainage channels had to be dug to lead off the surplus water and some of these channels gave their names to adjacent dwellings.

The place-names Goat (Farm) Cu, Sx and Goit (Lane) Nt, YW are derived from OE *gota*, 'a channel or stream' and it is possible that Gout(s) Gl, although it is first met in later records, had the same origin and meaning. Old French *goule*, 'throat', was borrowed in Middle English, giving Goole YW with an extension of meaning to 'ditch'; and the diminutive Old French *goulet* is the source of (The) Gullet Nth, Wa. A similar connotation of 'channel' occurs in Cut(t)mill Gl, O, Sr, Sx, Wa, Wo from Middle English *cut(te)*: and *cutel* gives Cuttle (Bridge) Wa, So and Cuttle (Brook) Wa. In the Cutmill names there is reference to an artificial millstream, a 'cut', which in ON was *rás*, literally 'a rush (of water)'. The common phrase '(a mill-) race', sometimes in use as a minor place-name, goes back to this ON word.

The usual term in OE for an artificial drainage channel was *dīc*, 'ditch', which is to be seen in place-names all over the map of England. The many Dittons were farms situated near ditches. Diss Nf and Dishforth YN (*ford*) show the effects of Anglo-Norman speech and the form Dyke, which is commonest in the Danelaw, is probably due to the influence of the ON *dík*, with the same meaning.

Some of the 'Dykes' and 'Ditches' on the modern map never held water; they were defensive. A bank was thrown up in digging a ditch and a wooden palisade was built along the crest of the bank. Some of these earthworks date back to the early Saxon period and were probably defended tribal boundaries; but the fact that some of them were attributed to the pagan god *Wōden* (eg Wansdyke W) or to *Grīm*, the same god under a by-name (eg Grim's Ditch or Dyke Hrt, Mx, O, W, YW etc) or to the Devil (eg C, Sx) indicates that these defensive works were named long after their builders had been forgotten. Their size suggested to the Saxons that these great earthworks could have been constructed only by superhuman beings. The Cambridgeshire Devil's Dyke was at first called simply 'The Ditch' and later 'The Great Ditch'. Its attribution to the Devil does not appear in records until the later sixteenth century.

LANDING-PLACES

A landing-place on a river bank was commonly *hȳð* in Old English. There were many along the Thames, distinguished one from another by the goods handled at each or by the owner's name. Putney Lo was *Putta's hȳð* and Stepney Lo was *Stybba's*; lambs (*lamb*) were put ashore at Lambeth Lo and cattle (*hrȳðer*) at Rotherhithe Lo. Both of these latter places were convenient for moving the stock to the marshland pastures behind the river wall. At Chelsea Lo limestone was landed for marling the rich arable fields of the neighbourhood and possibly because of the white dust at the wharf, it was called 'chalky' (OE *celce*). The place-names Hythe Ess, Ha, K, and Huyton La (with *tūn*), probably meant 'port' or 'haven'; like the riverine places, they provided facilities for the loading and unloading of boats.

A word with a similar meaning was OE *stæð*, as in Stafford St (with *ford*) and Stathe So. Names such as Staithes YN, Statham Ch (with the dative plural -*um*) and Croxteth La, '*Croc's* landing-place', are from the cognate ON *stǫð*. Later, Old French *kay* was borrowed as Middle English *key*, 'quay, wharf', giving such names as Key (Street) K, Wo, Quay (Street) frequent, Kew Sr, Newquay Co and Torquay D, 'the quay below the hill (OE *torr*)'.

An embankment or wharf was OE *hwearf*, as in Wharton We and Wherstead Sf (with *stede*, 'a place'). But Wharton He, La and Warton St, Wa were farms beside which grew swaying trees (*wæfre*). This latter OE term is also exemplified in Wavertree La. Wharton L and Warton La, Nb were farms, or perhaps enclosures in this context, where watch (OE *weard*) was kept for approaching armies or bands of marauders. Usually, the watching-places were situated on hills in order to afford a wider outlook, as in Warden Bd, Du, K, Nb (with *dūn*, 'hill') or Wardle Ch, La (with *hyll*) or Wardlow Db (with *hlāw*, 'hill').

MARSH

Many places that were once on the edge of marshes, or on islands in their midst, are now surrounded by firm, dry land, mainly as a result of the countless minor drainage works referred to in the previous section. The commonest word in earlier usage was OE *mersc*, from which our word 'marsh' is directly derived. It is related to *mere* (p 68) and to Latin *mare*, 'the sea'. Uncompounded, it is Marsh Bk, Sa, Sx or Merske YN. Numerous Marstons and Merston K, Sx, Wt refer to farms situated close to stretches of marshy land and Saltmarsh Gl, Sx, YE are in coastal areas, usually where the sea is slowly receding. Almost equally common is the place-name Fenton, in which the first element is OE *fenn*, 'a fen or marsh', though in northern names such as Fenby L (with ON *bý*, 'a farm') and Fenwick Nb, YW (with *wīc*, 'building(s)') we may have ON *fen*.

There are several other words, though of less frequent occurrence, which have closely similar meanings to *mersc* and *fenn*. The Welsh word *cors*, 'marsh, bog', gives Corse Gl, So, Wo, Corsley W ('marsh-clearing') and Cosford Sf. OE *snæp*, 'boggy land', is the origin of Snap Sx, W and of Snape D, Sf, Sx, W; but Snape La, Nt, YN, YW—all in northerly counties—is probably derived from a word related to Icelandic *snap*, which meant 'a patch of scanty grass for sheep to nibble at in snow-covered fields' or, more simply, 'poor pasture' (p 40). Another word for 'bog, swamp' was OE *sug(g)a*, which is found in Sugden Sa (with *dūn*), 'a hill') and Sugden YW (with *denu*, 'a valley'). Sugwas He has OE *wæsse*, also meaning 'swamp', as its second element, but the first could possibly be a bird-name *sucga* '(hedge) sparrow' or even a personal name *Sucga*, such as occurs in Sugworth Brk, '*Sucga*'s enclosure'.

The term *wæsse*, mentioned in the previous paragraph, is a noun related to the adjective 'wet'. It occurs in Washbourne Gl, with *burna*, 'brook'; in Alrewas St, with *alor*, 'alder-tree(s)'; in Broadwas Wo, with *brād*, 'wide'; and in Buildwas Sa, with the rare word *gebyldu*, 'building'. And the word 'wet' itself (OE *wēt*) is the first element of Wetton St, 'damp hill (*dūn*)' and Weetwood Nb, YW. The cognate ON *vátr*, 'wet', gives Watton YE (*tūn*) and Waitby We (*bý*). Another ON term, *mýrr*, 'mire, swamp', is the source of the second syllable in Redmires Du, of which the first was OE *hrēod*, 'reed(s)'; and in Walmer La, the first being OE *wald*, 'a forest'. On the other hand, Walmer K was 'the pool (*mere*) of the serfs or Britons (*walh*)'. The curious names (The) Wish K, R, Sx and Wiske YN go back to an OE *wisce*, 'a marshy meadow', which is also the origin of the second element of Dulwich Lo, 'the marshy meadow in which dill (OE *dile*) grows'. For ON *kjarr*, 'marsh overgrown with brushwood' or simply 'marsh', see p 56.

MUD

Nowadays farmyards and field-entries are often very muddy places, but in Saxon and medieval times almost everywhere that men and beasts frequently trod was deep in mire, for paving or metalling of ways was rare. The word 'mud' itself, OE *mudde*, is infrequently used in the names of places, but OE *sol* occurs occasionally, as in Sole Street and Solton (*tūn*) K and Sollom Cu, the latter in the dative plural; 'at the wallowing-places' is a possible meaning for this Cumberland name, though 'mud' and 'slough' are the more usual meanings. The original of 'slough' is OE *sloh* and it is found in Slough Bd, Bk, Sx. OE *slīm*, as in Slimbridge

Gl and Slimford Co, D had the meaning 'mud, slime' and OE *slæp*, a noun related to the modern verb 'to slip', survives in Islip Nth, 'a slippery place by the River Ise', and Ruislip Mx, in which it is combined with OE *risc*, 'rush(es)'.

Yet another term for 'mud' was OE *wāse*, a word related to *wisce* (p 75). The River Ouse Sx and the Ouse (Brook) Wa were 'muddy streams'. The (Great) Ouse and (Yorkshire) Ouse may go back to a word-root of a language used in Britain even before Celtic.

Old Norse *saurr* also meant 'mud' as well as 'dirt' and 'sour ground'; and it is cognate with OE *sūr*, 'sour'. In place-names, *saurr* is the source of the first element in the many Sowerbys of the northern counties, where ON *leirr*, 'mud, clay', is also found in such names as Lair (Hills) L, YE and Layerthorpe YE, the latter having the meaning 'farm, hamlet or village (ON *þorp*) situated on mud or clay'. The place is, in fact, on boulder clay, which is of glacial origin and very variable in the texture of its soils.

CHAPTER 5

The Countryside

Almost all early English place-names were given to natural or man-made features of the countryside, for the Anglo-Saxons were not town-dwellers by tradition or choice and the ruins of Romano–British towns were occupied, if at all, in the century following the conquest. Such archaeological evidence as there is, and it is very sparse, suggests that the towns functioned in much the same way as contemporary villages. The attraction was the surrounding fields rather than those houses that could be patched up and made habitable.

Many of the place-names considered in earlier chapters are rural in every sense; but this chapter is almost entirely concerned with the handiwork of man and with his modification of the landscape in wringing a livelihood from the soil—his fields and enclosures and his inroads into the wilderness.

There are several dozens of Old English terms for an enclosure and it is not easy to distinguish how one kind may have differed from another. Perhaps the commonest of all words in our place-names is *tūn*, of which we have already had many examples. Its earliest meaning had been 'fence' or 'hedge', which the German cognate, *Zaun*, still has. The meaning then evolved to 'that which is surrounded by a hedge or fence', namely 'an enclosure'. Names like Appleton and Pyrton (p 51) exemplify this sense, for they were 'apple- or pear-tree enclosures', that is, 'orchards'. The next development of meaning was to 'an enclosure with a dwelling', then 'a farmstead'; and as these gathered round them further dwellings and outbuildings, housing slaves or the farmer's offspring, the sense 'hamlet' and then 'village' or 'manor, estate' grew up. The modern meaning 'town' arises only in medieval times; and in place-names it commonly occurs in compounds such as Newtown Ha, Nb, Wt. Newton, on the other hand, which is found about 128 times on the map with various prefixes or affixes, usually indicates a 'new farm or hamlet' or even a village of late Saxon or early medieval settlement. The Newtowns were urban foundations of the thirteenth century, established by king, great noble or bishop as a market centre from which valuable dues could be collected.

And there are some other significant compounds of *tūn*. A grass enclosure or paddock was *gærs-tūn*, a common field-name as well as the minor name, Garston Ha, Hrt; and *lēac-tūn*, literally 'a leek-enclosure' or 'herb-garden', survives in various forms such as Leighton Bd, Ch, Ha, K, Sa, So, Laughton L (near Gainsborough), Lei, Sx and Latton Ess. From *bere-tūn*, 'a barley-enclosure' or 'corn farm', later 'an outlying barn for storing the lord's grain', we get many Bartons, some of them with prefixes such as Earl's Barton Nth or affixes such as Barton Regis Gl, besides Surbiton Sr, 'the south (*sūð*) barton', or Soberton Ha with the same origin and meaning.

The term *worð* also meant 'enclosure', but how it differed from a *tūn* is not clear. Place-names such as Hurworth Du, 'hurdle (OE *hurð*) enclosure' and Shuttleworth La, 'enclosure with a bar or bolt (OE *scytel*)' suggest a surrounding fence; but the nearest we can get to its early OE connotation is 'an enclosed space'. Many instances of the use of *worð* indicate it as a personal possession. Isleworth Mx (*Gīslhere*), Padworth Brk (*Peada*) and Wandsworth Lo (*Wændel*) are instances and they may imply an enclosure round the man's homestead, rather like a *topt* ('toft', p 118). But *worð* may be compounded with almost any other kind of word: Tamworth St (from the River Tame), Farnworth La (*fearn*, 'fern'), Butterworth La, YW (*butere*, 'butter') and very many more. It occurs uncompounded as Worth Ch, Do, K, So, Sx. The word *worð* is found in seventh-century documents, but not in later Old English as a common noun, which suggests that by then the term *worð* had ceased to be a living part of the language. Many of the places called *worðs* are still lone, remote homesteads; others evolved into hamlets or villages—a development comparable with that of many a *tūn*.

OE *worðig* meant the same as *worð*, but it is largely confined to the south-western shires as in Worthy D, Gl, Ha, W, Selworthy So (*sele*, 'a willow copse') and Fernworthy D (*fearn*). And another derivative, *worðign*, is typically a name-element of the West Midlands: Bredwardine He (OE *brerd*, 'hillside') and Leintwardine He, 'enclosure beside the River Lent'. (See pp 118–19.)

There is, too, a group of several related Old English words for 'enclosure' from which many existing place-names are derived. The commonest by far is (*ge-*)*hæg*, 'a fence or area enclosed by a fence'. In the Middle Ages it was often written in the Latinised form *haia*, and by then had acquired the more specialised meaning of 'part of a forest enclosed for hunting'; and it is most frequently met in old forested regions and is typical of them. This word, or possibly *hēg*, 'hay' or *hege*, 'hedge or fence', is found in Haydon Do, So, W (with *dūn*) and Hayton Cu, Nt, Sa (with *tūn*). The word *hæg* is more certainly the origin of the first syllable in Haywood He, Nt, St and of Hay He, We, Hayes D, Do, Wo and the frequent Devonshire minor name Hayne. In Woodhay Bk, Ha, Haywood is reversed—an unusual occurrence with place-names elements. In Oxhey Hrt, Wo there must have been an enclosed pasture for oxen. Heywood La was the 'high (OE *hēah*) wood'.

Hayne(s) K, Bd, L are from *hægen*; the cognate ON *hegn* is the source of Hainslack La, which may be rendered 'enclosure in a small shallow valley' (Old West Scandinavian *slakki*). The related ON *hegning* lies behind Haining Nb, Henning Cu, Nt and Heynings L, which all originally referred to 'enclosed land'.

Another word in this group, OE *haga*, underwent modifications of meaning from 'a hedge, an enclosure' to 'that which was enclosed', 'a messuage, a property'. This change in meaning is somewhat similar to those of *tūn* and *worð*. The cognate ON *hagi* developed a different specialised sense: 'a grazing enclosure, a pasture'. From the latter are derived Haigh La, YW, Haugh L and Hough L. Thornhough Nt was probably 'thorn-enclosure'. OE *haga* gives Haw Gl, O and Northaw Hrt, Newhaw Sr. The hedge (OE *hecg*) which surrounded many enclosures is referred to in numerous minor names such as Gutteridge Mx, which was sufficiently large (*grēat*) to be distinctive and Elsage Bk, which was presumably composed of elder trees (OE *ellen*).

The pound, a fenced plot into which strayed animals were put, may even now be in use in a few remote places and one still survives even in London, on Putney Heath. The word is related to 'pond', an artificially-created pool, and to some other terms shortly to be mentioned. Poundstock Co was a place (*stoc*) where there was a pound (*pund*) and Punda YE was a pound-enclosure (*haga*). Pound (Farm), and the like, is to be found in many counties. The overseer of the pound was called a 'pinder' (OE *pundere*) and his calling is commemorated in the place-name Poundisford So. OE *pynd*, the mutated form of *pund*, meaning either 'pound' or 'pond', occurs in Penn K, Pen (Hill) Sx, Piend D and Pin (Green) Hrt; and *pundfald*, 'a pinfold' or 'pound', also common in minor names, survives in Pinfold Nb and Poundfield Sx.

The OE word *penn*, 'a small enclosure, a pen', is of obscure origin, but possibly related to OE *pinn*, 'a pin, a peg'; and a *penn* may have been an enclosure that could be fastened with pin or peg. Hackpen (Hill) D, W may take their names from pens that had hooks (OE *haca*) for fastening the gates, though the second element may well have been British *penno-*, 'a hill', giving the sense 'hook-shaped hill'. From the British word come Penn (Hill) So, St and Penhill YN and names such as Pendle Hill and Pendlebury La. On the other hand, Penn Bk and Pann Wt are from OE *penn*; and so are Owlpen Gl, with the personal name *O(l)la* and Ipplepen D, with the name *Ip(p)ela*. A diminutive of this word, *pennuc*, is the source of Pinnock(s) Ha, Gl, W, 'a small pen' and another derivative, *penning*, 'a cattle enclosure', is common as the minor name Penning(s) in Wiltshire and less frequently in Gloucestershire. The latter word must be distinguished from OE *pen(d)ing*, 'a penny' (compare German *pfennig*), which is used in place-names of land on which a penny rent was payable. The manors or farms (*tūn*) of Pennington Ha, La and the messuage (ON *topt*) of Pennytoft L paid such a due.

Another small enclosure for animals, a fold (OE *fal[o]d*) is commonest in the south-eastern counties. Alfold Sr was an old (*eald*) one and the one at Slinfold Sx was on a slope (*slind*). The owner's name distinguished Dunsfold Sr (*Dunt*) from neighbouring folds. In Cowfold K, Sr, Sx we have an indication of the particular use of the enclosure and a *stōd-fald* was one in which horses were kept. Stotfold Bd, Du and Statfold St are instances. Stutfall (Castle) K had been one of the Roman forts guarding the 'Saxon Shore'; in Saxon times, if its contemporary name be a true guide to its use, it became a stud (*stōd*). Similarly, a *dēor-fald* was an enclosure for deer. This compound survives as Deerfold Wo, Durfold Co, Sr and Dorfold Ch.

There was, however, a quite distinct term for a sheepfold, *eowestre*. The first element of this word is *eowu*, 'a ewe', and the second seems sometimes to exist independently as *ēstre*, though it is, in fact, a development of the whole compound, after the loss of the 'w'. Austerfield YW and Nosterfield YN have *feld*, 'open country' as their final element; and Nosterfield has the 'n' of Middle English *atten* attached to it. (See p 65.) Osterley Mx and Ousterley Du are compounds with *lēah*, 'clearing'. High and Good Easter Ess were also the sites of sheepfolds. 'High' is higher, topographically, than 'Good' and 'Good' was originally '*Godgiefu*'s sheepfold', which is a woman's name, usually rendered in modern English as 'Godiva'.

The concept of a fold could also be expressed by the term *loc(a)*, of which the basic idea was a 'lock or bolt' and, in later use, 'an enclosure that could be locked'. Laughton L (near Folkingham), Lockwood YN, originally with ON *viðr*, 'a wood', and Lockwood YW, with OE *wudu*, as well as Porlock So, 'the enclosure by the harbour (OE *port*), contain this word. Letchworth Hrt has OE *lycce*, a mutated form of *loc*; its meaning was probably 'farm (*worð*) in an enclosure', for *worð* can hardly have

81

had its primary meaning of 'enclosure' if the whole was to make sense.

The OE term *tēag*, 'a small enclosure', sometimes gives rise to strange modern forms. Grafty K was a 'grass (*gærs*) enclosure', Olantigh K was distinguished by a holly tree (*holegn*) and Tilty Ess had a 'good or useful (*til*) enclosure'. The mutated form *tīege* is the source of Great, Little and Marks Tey Ess. The *Merk* family held the manor that bears their name in the earlier Middle Ages.

Parham Sx, with *hām*, 'homestead', and Parr La are derived from OE *pearr(e)*, 'an enclosure' and its diminutive *pearroc*, 'a paddock', is the source of Paddock (Wood) K and Parrock (Farm) K. Parrox La is from the same OE word and Parkham D is a compound of it with *hamm*, which had various meanings including 'an enclosure, meadow or water-meadow'. The Old French word *park*, 'an enclosed stretch of land for beasts of the chase', is a very common element in place nomenclature, for almost every parish has its great house and surrounding park. The term was taken into Old French from West Germanic and is of the same lineage as OE *pearroc*. The Old North French *plessis* 'an enclosure made with interlaced ('pleached') fencing', is the origin of Plessey Nb and Pleshey Ess; its derivative *plaissiet* gives Plashet(t) Ess, Sr, Sx and Plassett Nf. And yet another Old French word, *clos*, is the source of many field-names such as Cow Close and Rough Close. The cathedral 'closes' at, for instance, Winchester and Salisbury, are quite literally enclosures with the medieval walls and gateways still surviving.

Another park-like enclosure was an *edisc*. The word occurs in Edgefield Nf (*feld*) and Edgeley Ch, Sa (*lēah*); Escombe Du was the dative plural of the uncompounded form, meaning 'at the parks'. Brockdish Nf has *brōc*, 'stream', as first element; Farndish Bd was a 'ferny (*fearn*) park'; Standish Gl, La was stony (*stān*) or its walls were of stone; Cavendish Sf was '*Cāfna*'s or *Cāfnōð*'s park'. The Sussex place-names Glynleigh (*lēah*) and Glynde(bourne) have OE *glind* as first element, meaning 'fence or enclosure', the first in a wood or clearing (*lēah*), the second by a

82

stream (*burna*). The same meanings existed for the OE and ON word *spenning*, from which are derived Spennithorne YN, 'thorn (*þorn*) enclosure' and Spennymoor Du, 'enclosure on a moor (*mōr*)'.

In place-names of rather later formation the term OE *geard*, 'a fence, enclosure, yard', is found. It is frequent in field-names and enters into a few major names such as Bromyard He, with *brōm*, 'broom' or Rudyard St, in which the first element is the rare OE *rūde*, the shrub 'rue', botanically *Rūta graveolens*, indigenous in southern Europe and a valuable simple. The ON form *garðr*, 'enclosure', is also common in field-names and is found in major names like Applegarth YE, YN, which corresponds to the southern English Appleton, 'an orchard', and in Vinegarth YE, which is matched by the mainly southern name Vineyard(s) and Winyard W. A possible borrowing from the Latin *vinitorium*, 'a vineyard', is OE *winter* in the place-name Midwinter D, which would have meant 'the middle vineyard', or Radwinter Ess, which probably had as first element the woman's name *Rǣdwynn*. A modern German place-name such as Königswinter, among the Rhineland vineyards, is probably a similar instance of a borrowing from the Latin word, and it meant 'the king's vineyard'.

Although Appleton, literally 'apple enclosure', in effect meant 'orchard', the ancestor of the latter word, OE *ort-geard*, was used in the formation of place-names. The first element *ort* was from Latin (*h*)*ortus*, 'a garden'. Orchard Co, D, So are obvious derivatives of this compound; Orcheton D has it with *tūn* and Orchardleigh So with *lēah*.

A plot of enclosed land in the marshes was OE *hop*, as in Hopton Sf. However, the more usual meaning of this term was 'a small enclosed valley', as in Hopton Db, He, Sa, St, YW, Hopwood La, Wo, the very common place-name Hope and numerous other compounds such as Bramhope YW, with *brōm*, or Worksop, which was '*Werc*'s or *Wyrc*'s enclosed valley'. The diminutive *hoppet* is found in the field-names of some counties, as for instance, Hoppits in the parish of Bovingdon Hrt. Finally in

Cumberland and on the Welsh marshes, Old Welsh *lann* occurs in areas where the two languages existed for a long time side by side. Originally meaning 'enclosure', especially one for Christian worship, it attracted burials to its hallowed ground and later a church was usually built within it. A few instances of its use are: Landican Ch (dedicated to a St *Tecan*), Landkey D (St *Cai*), Llanwarne He, 'church by the swamp or alders (Welsh *gwern*)', and Llanmynech Sa, 'church of the monks (Welsh *mynech*)'. The Cornish word *lan*, which had the same meaning, is the source of names such as Launceston, 'enclosure by an elder-copse (Old Cornish *scawet*)' and Lamellan, '*Maylwen*'s church'.

Away from the marshes, a high cross, usually of wood, marked the place of worship. Such a cross (OE *māēl*) gave its name, in the earliest Christian period, to places such as Malden Sr, Maldon Ess, Mauldon Bd and Meldon Nb, all of which have *dūn* as second element, suggesting that the cross was erected in a prominent position. Very many of our village churches are situated on knolls close to the nucleus of the old settlements and some of them are probably successors to high crosses. Another OE word *līc-tūn*, literally 'corpse enclosure' (as in Litchadon D), refers to a burial-ground corresponding to a *lan(n)*. This would no doubt have been the 'field church' in use before the local thegn built a timber or stone church, usually on the same site. The place-name Woodchurch Ch, K refers to a timber building; Whit-church Bk, D, Do, Ha, He, O, Sa, So probably commemorates the whiteness of new stone buildings, many of limestone or hard chalk (clunch). Other early timber structures are implied by the place-names Berechurch Ess (*bred*, 'a plank', metathesised to *berd*), and Stokenchurch Bk (*stoccen*, 'made of logs'). The last of these names describes the nave of the Saxon church at Green-stead-juxta-Ongar Ess, built of split sections of oak trunks.

GATES

Enclosures, large or small, need gates, especially those for confining animals. The word *geat*, 'gap, gate', became *yate* in the singular in Middle English—hence Yate Gl, Yateley Ha (*lēah*), Yatton He, W, 'farm near a gap in the hills' and Yates-bury W, 'fort (*burh*) near a gap' or '*Geat*'s fort'. In Burgate Ha, Sf, Sr we have the probable meaning 'fort-entrance' and in the Kentish names Margate, Ramsgate, Kingsgate and Sandgate the meaning of the second element is 'gap in the sea-cliffs'. The first element of Margate was *mere*, 'the sea'; of Ramsgate it was the personal name *Hræfn*; and Kingsgate commemorates a landing by Charles II in 1683 and is a much later place-name coinage than the others. Sandgate is situated on the geological formation called the Lower Greensand.

Specialised uses of OE *geat* are: *hlid-geat*, 'a swing-gate', as in Lidgate Co, Sf and Lydiate La, Wo; *hlīep-geat*, 'leap-gate', which allowed passage to deer but not to cattle. Examples of this word in the naming of places are Lipgate and Lipyeate, So, Lypiatt Gl, W, all in the South-West; and a further specialised use is *wind-geat*, which geographers call a 'wind-gap', giving Wingate D, Du, Nb, Sr, YW and Winnats (Pass) Db. The 'g' rather than 'y' in some modern forms is due to its quite normal occurrence in the Middle English plural of the noun.

The other common word for 'gate' was *hæcc*, usually referring to the entrance to a park or forest. Hatch Ha, So, W represents the modern form of this word. In Hackford Nf and Hackforth YN (also a *ford*-name originally) there is reference to a gate across a stream, presumably to confine animals to fields along its banks and prevent them from straying by crossing the ford.

FIELDS AND MINOR NAMES

The OE word *feld*, which is the source of modern 'field', had the meaning 'open country' and it was used in a contrasting manner with *wudu*, 'woodland', *dūn*, 'hill', and *fenn*, 'marshland'. The cognate Dutch word *veldt* retains the meaning 'open country' and was used by the Boer settlers of southern Africa in the sense 'treeless (uplands)'. In England, *feld* occurs most commonly in old forested regions like The Weald of the South-East; and in such regions *lēah*, 'clearing' is also common. As the woodland areas were later in settlement, the meaning 'forest' is less likely unless it referred to a broad tract of country. Both *lēah* and *feld* were probably applied to either natural or to man-made clearings, but it is fairly certain that a *feld* was more extensive than a *lēah*, for Enfield (Chase) Mx (*Ēana*'s open country), a royal hunting ground, stretched for miles and Hatfield (Chase) YW (healthy [*hǣd*] 'open country'), is still reckoned to be of 180,000 acres.

Hatfield is a name that occurs in many counties; heathland is usually treeless so that *feld* was an apt description of it. And marshland, too, is often treeless. Maresfield Sx and Marshfield Gl both have OE *mersc* as first element. Moreover, the 'open country' was sometimes characterised by the domestic animals pastured on it, as for instance, Rotherfield Ha, O, Sx, which supported cattle (*hrīðer*) or Sheffield Sx, where sheep (*scēap*) predominated. Later names like Cowfield or Horsefield are fairly common. Chesterfield Db, St was 'open country near or belonging to a (Roman) fortification (OE *ceaster*)' and Sheffield YW was 'open country beside the River Sheaf'. The modern meaning of 'field' probably developed after the mid-fourteenth century, when open country began to be divided up and enclosed as the fields that we are familiar with today.

In Anglo-Saxon times a plot of arable was called an *æcer*; ON *akr* is indistinguishable from it in place-names. Acre Nf represents the uncompounded use of this word. Many compounds of it occur with a crop-name as prefix, as for example, Benacre K, Sf, with *bēan*, 'bean' and Linacre(s) Db, Gl, La, Nb etc, with *līn*, 'flax'. Most of these are minor names, usually field-names. A cultivation terrace, OE *hlinc*, such as may still be seen on the steeper flanks of the chalk downs of southern England, survives in names such as Linch Sx, Link Wo and Lintz Du, as well as in compounds like Linkenholt Ha, with *holt*, 'a wood' or Standlynch W, with *stān*, 'stony'. The modern word 'lynchet', as applied to the ancient terraces on the downs, appears to be no older than the late eighteenth century, though obviously related to *hlinc*.

Even in early times there were some enclosed fields. Before the English migration to Britain the Latin word *campus* was borrowed and became OE *camp*, a word found mainly among the place-names of the South-East. However, Campden Gl is an exception in the West Country. It meant 'valley (denu) with an enclosed field'. Most Comptons were valley (*cumb*) farms (*tūn*), but Compton Db has *camp* as first element. Examples from the main region of distribution are: Addiscombe Sr, '*Æddi*'s *camp*' and Swanscombe K, which was 'the herdsman's (*swān*) or *Swān*'s *camp*'.

But many fields, enclosed or not, were under grass. *Anger*, 'a pasture', is the source of Ingram Nb, with *hām*, 'a homestead'; and Angram, which is from the dative plural of *anger*, occurs in Lancashire and several times in Yorkshire. Its literal meaning was 'at the pastures'. A field of grass for mowing and for the making of hay, 'a meadow', was OE *mǣd*, a word related to *māwan*, 'to mow' and to *mǣð*, 'the cutting of grass', which survives as the last syllable of our word 'aftermath'. The modern word 'meadow', is from the oblique cases, as for example, the genitive and dative singular *mǣdwe*. 'Mead', from the nominative singular, also survived in common usage until recent centuries. In place-names we have Medbourne Lei, W, with *burna*, 'a stream' and Runnymede Sr, a compound of *rūn*, 'council' with *ēg*, 'island' and *mǣd*. It is quite possible, however, that the name was originally *rūningemǣd*, 'meadow where councils were held' and that the famous meeting of 1215, when the barons extorted Magna Carta from the reluctant King John, was not the first council held in the meadow.

In field-names a considerable variety of words for 'a plot, a piece of land' existed, though they seldom appear in the names of villages. OE *stycce*, cognate with German *Stück*, meant 'a piece (of land)' and survives in such field-names as The Stitches C. OE *sticce*, on the other hand, is of doubtful meaning, though 'a balk' (an unploughed strip between holdings in the common field), is possible. It survives mostly in Wiltshire field-names as Stitch or its derivative Stitching, though instances of it occur in other and widely separated counties (eg Nt, O, YW). OE *plot* was also widely used, as in Plot(s) Farm Nt and the field-name Plot YW; and its secondary form, *plat*, is found in Middle English from the thirteenth century onwards in names such as Platt Wo or Burnt, Hard, Holly and Marsh Platt(s) YW. Furthermore, ME *plek*, which has an identical form in Dutch, occurs as (The) Pleck He, Bull Plecks and Busky (ON *buskr*, 'bush') Pleck YW. It too meant 'a small piece of ground'; and ME *splott*, which is related to the word 'spot', is found as (The) Splatt(s) D, O. Finally, Old French *pece*, 'a plot of land', is frequent in field-names such as No Man's Piece, Church Piece and Poors Piece C.

There are certain words that recur in field-names simply because they described features of common occurrence. The balk (OE *balca*) survives as The Balk(s), Moor Balk C, Rowebalk Bd (OE *rūh*, 'rough') and many more. In Middle English *butte* described the strip of land adjoining a boundary in the common fields; But Hill Wa and Laithbutts La, YW (ON *leið*, 'a track'), are from this word. A distinct term, Old French *butt*, 'a mound', especially one for archery practice, is found in names like Robin Hood's Butts Cu, He, So; and there is a third *butt*, this one from Old English, meaning 'a tree stump', which explains names such as Burnt Butts YE and Budbridge Wt, which was a bridge made of logs, presumably not unlike a Stockbridge (p 92).

A mound marking a boundary, OE *ball*, is referred to especially in field-names of the south-western shires and in Oxfordshire, often surviving in unchanged form, as in Ball Down and Ball Hill Copse W. A triangular plot or a point of land, OE *gāra*, occurred at the sides of irregularly-shaped open fields. Some examples of the use of this term are: Gore W, Kensington Gore Lo (a triangular extension of the parish of Kensington into the City of Westminster), Bredgar K (*brād*, 'broad'), and Langar Nt (*lang*, 'long'). In Gargrave YW, we may have the word in its original meaning, 'a spear', and the place-name would then have meant 'wood (*grāf*) from which spear-shafts were cut'.

A stretch of land, *grund*, survives as Ground or, in the plural, (New) Grounds Gl. Stanground Hrt was 'stony' (*stān*) and a fort (*burh*) existed at Grundisburgh Sf. The ON *flat* had a similar meaning, though with an emphasis on the flatness of the ground. Shortflatt Nb (OE *sceort*) and Tarn Flat La (ON *tjǫrn*) are self-evident in total meaning. But curious names, far from obvious, have evolved from ON *fit*, 'grassland on a river-bank', which is fairly common in the field-names of the Danelaw. For instance, the Cumberland names Cold Fitz and Lambfoot or Fitts YN, YW have no apparent topographical connotation in their modern forms. Lambfoot is, in fact, a development from *lang* ('long') *fit*. On the other hand, Old Danish *klint* survives in the dialect word 'clint' which referred to 'a hard rock projecting from the side of a hill or from a river bank' and in minor names as Clint(s) Nb, YN, YW, though those ignorant of the dialect could hardly guess at the meaning.

Another word in many minor names is OE *slæd*, 'a valley', occurring on the map as (The) Slad(e) Db, Gl, La, Lo, O, YW etc; but Sleddale We, YN, in which it is combined with *dæl*, 'valley', suggests that *slæd* had some special connotation now lost. The word 'stile' (OE *stigel*) is also fairly common in forms such as Steel(e) Nb, Sa or Stile Cu. It is moreover, the origin of the first element in Stilton Hu.

Finally, in most shires there are numerous reproachful names for barren ground. One of the commonest words involved is OE *hungor*, 'hunger', as in the many Hunger or Hungry (*hungrig*) Hills, in Hungerton L, Lei and in Hungerford Brk, which may originally have referred to a river-crossing leading to infertile fields. A small selection of contemptuous field-names of the West Riding of Yorkshire will illustrate their variety: Break Back, Cover Beggar, Dear Bought, Dismal, Labour in Vain, One Too Many, Picket Pocket, Poverty and Painful, Spendthrift and Wearasome [*sic*]. The converse is implied by names such as Full Belly Dale, Goodnatured Flat, Honey Pot and Paradise, though in fact some of these names may have been used ironically of very poor land.

THE SETTLEMENT OF THE EMPTY LANDS

The first phase of Anglo-Saxon colonisation in Britain was generally in regions that had been cultivated for long before the arrival of the English tribes in this country. The earliest period of expansion from the regions of primary settlement may well be represented by place-names such as Wokingham Brk, 'homestead (*hām*) of *Wocc*'s people', which was a secondary settlement from Woking Sr, 'the people of *Wocc*'; and it is possible that Wokefield, '*Wocc*'s open country' may belong to a still later phase of colonisation (p 140).

As we saw earlier, the word *feld* was probably applied to natural open country or to that which had been cleared before the English invasions. Anglo-Saxon 'felling' could also have produced a *feld* (these two words are related) if it were extensive enough for the word to be applied to it; or if it were smaller, it could be called a *lēah*, 'clearing'. Both *lēah* and *feld* are very common elements in place-names, especially those of old forest country. The Weald (OE *weald*, 'forest') of the South-East has numerous examples: Surrey as a whole has more than fifty names in *feld* and about 110 in *lēah*; Sussex has seventy in *feld* and over 120 in *lēah*. Some, at any rate, of these place-names arose as a result of deliberate forest clearance for cultivation. An expanding population required ever larger acreages of arable to support its needs.

The OE term (*ge-*)*fall*, 'a forest clearing', is also related to *feld* and to the verbs 'to fall' and 'to fell'. It is the origin of the second element of Threlfall La, 'clearing of the serfs (ON *prǽll*) and of Woodfall La (with OE *wudu*, 'a wood'). Of similar meaning is a group of related words which imply 'ridding (the ground of trees)'. OE *roð* was a place 'rid of trees'; in Rothwell L, Nth, YW there was a spring or stream (OE *wella*) in the clearing thus made, but Rothley Lei, Nb probably has *lēah* in its older sense of 'wood', for this name can hardly have meant 'clearing in a clearing'. Yet the later sense of *lēah* is obviously needed in

90

Woodleigh D, Gl and Woodley(s) Gl, O, in which *wudu* and *lēah* are combined. In fact, Rothley and Woodley had the same meaning: 'clearing in a wood'. OE *rȳd* and its variants give names such as Rede K, Sx; and (*ge-*)*rydd* is the source of Ridley Ch, Nb, which is directly comparable in meaning with Rothley; *rydding* lies behind Reading K and *ryden* or *reden* gives Reading Ess. Reading Brk is a much more ancient name, belonging, like Woking, to the earliest period of colonisation and meaning 'people of *Rēad(a)*' (p 138).

A fairly common term used in the place-names of Lancashire and Yorkshire, especially, is OE *rod(u)*. It forms the final element of Ackroyd YW, 'clearing among oaks' and of Woodroyd and Ormerod, both of which have personal names as their first elements. In Royd(s) and Rhode(s) we have *rod(u)* without a prefix. But the commonest word for 'clearing', at least in the northwestern shires, was *þveit*, which seems to have been applied especially to a clearing that became meadow land; and it continued to be used in the Middle Ages for newly-made clearings. In its simple form it has become Thwaite(s) Cu, Nf, Sf, YE, YN, YW; and of many compounds the following are perhaps the most interesting: Braithwaite Cu, YN, with ON *breiðr*, 'broad'; Langthwaite Cu, La, YN, with *lang*, 'long'; Huthwaite Nt, YN with *hōh*, 'a spur of land'; Crossthwaite Cu, We, YN, with Old Irish *cros*, 'a (stone) cross'; Thornthwaite Cu, We, YW, with *þorn*; Rosthwaite La, with ON *hross*, 'a horse' and very many more besides.

The methods of making clearings in the forest are illustrated in several types of name. Ring-barking of the trees in the winter would prevent the sap from rising in the spring so that they would die. At a suitable time in the following summer, after a spell of dry weather, the undergrowth would be fired and a burnt area remain, the soil enriched with potash and the accumulated humus of many autumn leaf-falls. OE *bærnet(t)* was such a 'burned' place; Barnet Hrt, Mx and Burnett So are from this word. OE *brand* had much the same meaning and survives in Brand Nt, Nth and in Brandred K, 'burned clearing (*rȳd*)'. The related *brende* or *brent* gives Brind YE and compound names such as Brandwood Wo, Brentwood Ess, Burntwood St or Brindley La, YN, the latter with *lēah*, 'a wood'. But Brant Broughton L, Brent Eleigh Sf and Brent Pelham Hrt were villages destroyed by fire.

The felling of trees with the axe is implied by OE *ge-fall* (p 90) and by ON *hǫgg*, a word cognate with our verb 'to hew'. The common north country name Hagg(s) La, Nb, YN, YE etc is from this ON term. And the residue of felling or burning was the stumps of trees, which could not easily be removed with the primitive equipment of colonists. They were constrained to sow seed in the spaces between the stumps. A clearing with stumps is no doubt usually implied in the many minor names that contain one of the several related words for 'a stump'. OE *stubb* occurs in Stub(House) Du, YW and in many other minor names, though the possibility cannot be excluded that such names may refer to only a single tree-stump or to the material of a building, rather than to stumps remaining in the ground. The collective noun, OE *stubbing*, as in Stubbing Nt, YN etc must, however, refer to more than one stump and is best rendered as 'a place from which trees have been cleared'; and the mutated form *stybbing* of Stibbington Hu meant the same. Yet another related word, *styfic*, 'a stump', is found in the names Steeton YW, Stewton L, both with *tūn*; in Stewkley Bk and Stukeley Hu with *lēah*, 'clearing'; in Stetchworth C (*worð*), Stiffkey Nf, with *ēg*, 'island'; and in Stivichall Wa, in which name it is compounded with *halh*, 'a corner of land'. Those with *lēah*, at any rate, refer to clearings with stumps.

The OE word *stocc* is less likely to have referred to the clearing of forest, but rather to the use of logs as building material in names such as Stockbridge Do, Ha, YW and to stumps set in the ground surrounding a spring in Stockwell Gl, He, Lo. The simple form Stock Bk, K, Wo similarly implied something made from one or more logs; but some of the Stockleighs and Stockleys D, Du, Sf etc were no doubt 'stump-clearings' rather than 'woods or clearings belonging to a *stoc*' ('a religious foundation' or 'a secondary settlement' or, simply, 'a place'). This word with one 'c' is the origin of the very common place-name Stoke. The collective term *stoccing* also meant 'a clearing with stumps' and is common in field-names as Stocking He, St, YN, YW etc and in minor names such as Stockingford Wa.

A more general term for 'new land taken into cultivation' was OE *brēc*, a noun related to the verb 'to break'. It is found frequently in the minor names of the midland counties as Breach; and in Breeches K. Bratton W was a farm established on new land. In later times, Old French *assart* was used instead of *brēc*, surviving in many field-names in forms like Sart D, the Sarts Nt. This word was the one commonly used in the records of the monasteries, the great lords and the clerics for the new clearings on their estates. They and their scribes were more at home in the French language than in English.

The expansion of the cultivated areas is also indicated on the modern map by several words that refer to land taken either into temporary or permanent cultivation. OE *innām*, literally 'taken in', has a second element related to OE *niman* and to modern German *nehmen*, 'to take'. Instances of its use are Inham(s) C, L and Inholms C, Nt, Sr, Sx. ON *intak* is, literally, 'intake' and is, in part, from the ON verb *táka*, whence comes our modern verb 'to take'. It is found as Intak(e) in the field-names of several northern counties. And much the same meaning was borne by ON *afnám*, related to *afnima*, 'to seize'. Apart from northern field-names, it is the source of Avenham La. Yet another common field-name, particularly of southern shires, is Innings K, Hrt, Ninnings Ess, Hrt, which are both derived from OE *inning*, 'a piece of land taken in or enclosed'. Finally, the word for 'an addition or increase', OE *ēcels*, was used in the sense of 'land added to an estate' and, usually, from the waste. Etchells Ch, Db and Nechells Sr, Wa are instances of its use in this sense.

TOPOGRAPHICAL WORDS

Every convolution of the ground had its name in Saxon times

and the more obvious surface features of the landscape were distinguished by descriptive words that were originally metaphorical. A sharp ridge or an escarpment was called an Edge Ch, Gl, Sa, from OE *ecg*, a term also used metonymously for the sword. Edgeworth La, Gl, was an enclosure (*worð*) near a scarp, the 'edge' of a line of hills. The back of a man or beast was OE *hrycg*, our word 'ridge', which is now commonly used topographically. Ridge Hrt, Rudge Gl, So represent variant dialectal developments of it. Sandridge D, Hrt and Ashridge refer, the first to the soil, and the second to the trees growing on it. Rugeley St was 'a wood or clearing on a ridge'. The cognate ON *hryggr* gives, for example, Rigton YW (*tūn*) and Brownrigg Cu. In the latter name we have ON *brún*, 'an edge or brow of a hill', which is cognate with OE *brū*, 'an eyebrow or brow of a hill', another instance of an extension of meaning into the metaphorical. This is exemplified by Mere Brow La, where 'brow of a hill' is obviously relevant.

OE *næss* or *ness* and ON *nes* or OE *nēs*, 'a promontory or headland' are all related to an ancient Germanic word-root for 'nose', represented by OE *nōs*. This last term occurs in Dunnose Wt, 'hill (*dūn*)-nose' and Hackness YN, 'hook (OE *haca*)-nose'. The other related words give rise to The Naze Ess, Neston Ch, Ness Ch, Sa, YN—all from *næss* or *ness*; and Neasden Mx (with *dūn*) and Nesbitt Nb (with OE *byht*, 'bend') from OE *nēs*; and Skegness L (with the ON personal name *Skeggi*) and Holderness YE (with ON *họldr*, 'a yeoman') from ON *nes*.

Hills are imagined as having the form of a hat or hood (related words) and were named accordingly. In instances such as Hatt Co, Ha, W, Hat Hill Sx we have OE *hæt(t)* used in this way. Hatley C, Bd, 'wood on or by a hat-shaped hill' is one of the rare compounds of this word. Similarly, Hood D, YN and Hotham YE, originally the dative plural in -*um*, are from OE *hōd*, 'hood'. There is metaphor, too, in the use of the term *byden*, 'a vessel or a tub', to describe a depression in the ground, as in Bedwell Bd, D, Nth, So, YW, all of which probably meant 'spring in a hollow'; but it is possible that the spring was actually provided with a tub, let into the ground to give extra depth for ease in drawing water. Stave-lined pits, which could have been tubs sunk below the surface of the ground, are known from the excavation of Anglo-Saxon sites. Bedford Sx, Bedfont Mx and Bedmond Hrt all have *byden* as first element, with *funta*, 'a spring', as ending, all of them having the same meaning as Bedwell. Wherwell Ha has OE *hwer*, 'a kettle', though the significance of this vessel in such a context is less obvious except we remember that 'kettle' was originally used of an open container for the boiling of water and that the shape of the depression in which the spring was situated was thought to resemble one. Kettlewell YW, with OE *cetel*, no doubt had a similar connotation. But the usual word for 'a hollow', OE *pytt*, though cognate with the Latin *puteus*, 'well, pit', is apparently never combined with *wella*; Pett K, Pitt Ha, Sandpits (a frequent minor name), and Stonepit(s) represent instances of this word as used in place-names. It could also be used of a trap for wild animals (see Wolpit, p 34).

Hills, woods or other features of the landscape that appeared circular, at any rate from some positions, occasionally had the word 'wheel' applied to them. OE *hweowol*, or in shortened form, *hwēol*, was used of a water-wheel, a curving hill or valley, or of almost anything round, such as a stone circle. Valleys are so characterised in Welldale and Wheeldale YN, and Wheldale YW, all with *dæl* and in Whielden Bk, with *denu*, 'valley'. Wheeldon Db, with *dūn* and Wellsborough Lei, Whilborough D, both with *beorg*, are descriptive of hills. Wheelton La and Whilton Nth were settlements that may have gained their names from either wheel-shaped hills or from water-wheels; or possibly they were ring-villages. (See Ringstead, below.)

A round-topped hill or a stone circle is also the secondary meaning of OE *hwerfel* and ON *hvirfill*, 'a circle'. Whorlton Cu, Nb, YN are perhaps comparable in meaning with Whilton above; Quarles Nf and Wharles La are developments from the nominative plural and probably referred to prehistoric monuments such as henges, disc barrows or other circular earthworks. The village-names Ringstead Do, Nf, Nth may well refer to the

kind of circular settlement defended by a ditch, bank and palisade, of which fragmentary remains sometimes survive (eg
Great Wolford Wa and Pleshey Ess, see pp 33, 82), though
neither of these names involves the word 'ring'. OE *hring* is the
source of our word 'ring' and the *stede* of Ringstead meant
simply 'place'. Ringmer Sx had a circular pool (*mere*); one called
Ring Mere survives on East Wretham Heath Sf. It gave its name
to a battle in which the Danes defeated the levies of Cambridgeshire in AD 1010. And ON *kringla*, meant the same as *hring*, but is
apparently unrelated. It gives such names as Cringledike Cu,
'ring-ditch' and Cringleford Nf, which is situated on an unre-
markable curve of the River Yare.

OE *trun*, or metathesised, *turn*, was an adjective that described
something round or something that turns. In Trumfleet YW it
was applied to a stream (OE *flēot*), in Turley YW to a wood
(*lēah*). Turnham (Green) Mx, YE are close to bends in a river
and Turndenn K was a 'round swine pasture' (OE *denn*). The related adjective, OE *trind*, of like meaning, gives Trenley K and
Tirley Gl, both circular woods or clearings; and the noun
trendel is the origin of the name (The) Trundle (Goodwood) Sx,
a roughly circular hill-fort of the Iron Age. Trentishoe D is by a
circular hill (*hōh*).

MISCELLANEOUS WORDS

This section of the chapter is a rag-bag of oddments that belong to no obvious category, yet include a number of commonly
occurring place-names elements that are of some interest.

Many a prominent hill-top, especially those in coastal regions,
is shown on the map as Beacon Hill Cu, Ess, He, Nt, Sf, Sr, Sx,
YW etc (OE *ge-bē[a]con*). Although few of these names are found
in records dating from before the sixteenth century, the names
were no doubt in use and the beacons fired many times in the
centuries before the sighting of the Spanish Armada in 1588.
French raids, such as those in 1377 and 1448 when Rye was
burnt down, or in 1359, 1380 and 1449 when Winchelsea was

sacked, required an 'early warning system' from look-outs posted on the nearest high ground. It so happens that no 'beacon' names survive at likely local spots in East Sussex, but many of the minor place-names of that county are as yet unpublished, including those to be found in early documents but which no longer exist on the map. Of course, once the beacons had gone out of use, the name, too, would sometimes disappear. The absence of beacon-names from the modern map of the region is certainly not proof of their never having existed there.

OE *cweorn*, 'a quern' or 'hand-mill', occurs in place-names that referred to quarries from which millstones were obtained. Every village needed to have them and to renew them when too far worn to be effective. Quarndon Db, Quorn(don) Lei, Quarrendon Bk and Quárrington Du begin with this word and ended with *dūn*, 'a hill'. Whernside YW was a hill-side (OE *sīde*) from which they were hewn. A wood in a similar position was OE *hangra*, which gives rise to the common Clayhanger Ch, D, St, Clehonger He and Clinger D., Gl—all with 'clay' (OE *clǣg*) as the first element. Bockhanger K was a 'beechwood (*bōc*) on a hill-side'; Gilbert White's Oakhanger Ha is self-evident, but Solinger Bk was 'a willow (*salh*)-wood on a hillside'.

'A steep place, a chasm, a leap' or 'a place only to be crossed by leaping' was OE *hlēp*. Lipe So, W are, presumably, at steep places; Birdlip Gl, as many motorists will remember, is on the steep scarp of the Cotswolds; literally it meant either 'bird (OE *bridd*)-leap' or 'bride (OE *brȳd*)-leap'. As with so many place-names, there is a highly imaginative touch in the first alternative; the second may enshrine the memory of some lost folk-tale or perhaps a minor historical incident that impressed itself on local consciousness. Hartlip K and Hindlip Wo, referring to deer, may retain a memory of some long-lost incident of the chase.

On the map of the northern counties one sees, here and there, a name containing the ending -scar. It is from ON *sker*, 'a rock, a reef, or a rocky cliff'. The last of these meanings is best illustrated by Giggleswick Scar YW. This meant '*Gicel*'s dairy-farm (OE *wīc*) by the rocky cliff'. The Scar runs from north-west to south-east as a wall of limestone from Settle to Ingleton. It is a geological fault, a dislocation and break in the rock-bedding, with one side of the break remaining higher than the other. Gordale Scar YW (OE or ON *gor*, 'dirt' and *dæl* or *dalr*, 'valley'), on the other hand, has the twin-facing limestone cliffs of a gorge, comparable with the famous one at Cheddar; and Ravenscar YN (ON *hrafn*) is so named from its tumbled sea-cliffs.

Finally, there is a word which suggests that our early ancestors were not entirely without aesthetic appreciation of the landscape, for they used *scēne*, 'bright, beautiful', for several landscape features. Shenley Bd, Bk, Hrt was such a woodland or clearing (*lēah*); Shenfield Ess was 'beautiful open country (*feld*)'; and Shenstone St had probably a 'bright' and therefore conspicuous, stone (*stān*). It is less easy to imagine what this word meant in relation to settlements (*tūn*), such as Sheinton Sa or Shenington O, though many early forms of the latter name suggest that it was, in fact, 'a beautiful hill (*dūn*)'.

CHAPTER 6

The Towns

For much of the time when place-names were first coming into use, the distinction between town and country was far less absolute than it usually is today. Almost all medieval English towns were no larger than present-day villages. In many ways the townsman was a villager and a countryman. Even towards the end of the eighteenth century a Londoner could stroll from Aldgate into the fields of Stepney, leaving the built-up area in about five minutes after passing Aldgate Pump; and even in this century cattle were still stalled within the City of London. In the Middle Ages, farmsteads and gardens were normal features in most towns and men went daily outside the walls to till the nearby fields.

The number of minor place-names surviving in all our towns and cities is enormous and only a few can be mentioned here. The various terms for a street are numerous. The word 'street' itself was used out in open country for a Roman road, giving many Stratfords and Strattons; and from late Saxon times it was used of an urban road, as it still is. In many towns the High Street is the 'chief' thoroughfare. In Edmonton Mx, the *Heghestrate* (1342) became the *Forestreete* by 1650 and the same happened in Trowbridge and in the town of Hertford. There, not surprisingly, Back Street was behind Fore Street. Furthermore, Back Lane occurs in many towns, eg Royston and Southwell.

Quite often the market place was also a main thoroughfare; Market Street, as in Newton Abbot and Tavistock, is a quite common name. In larger towns, markets were held more than once in the week and could be referred to as Monday Market (Street), Devizes; Wednesday Market, Beverley; Thursday Market, York and Saturday Market, Beverley. Chesterfield has a Weekday Market. Some markets were specialised in the wares sold; the commonest is the Cattle Market. Ipswich had a Butter Market, Bristol and Westminster a Hay Market, Norwich a Madder Market, where a plant yielding a reddish dye was on sale; and there was an Iron Market at Newcastle-under-Lyme. In Nottingham and Witney, butter was sold at the Butter Cross and there is a Poultry Cross in Salisbury. At Malmesbury and elsewhere is a Market Cross, the goods unspecified.

Horse Fairs were held in Cricklade, Malmesbury, Bristol, Leicester and Banbury, giving their names to parts of these and of other towns. Northampton had a Horse Market and Mare Fair. The word 'fair', which meant a gathering of merchants, is from Old French *feire*; 'market' was an earlier borrowing from the same source. But the Old English word for 'market' or 'market-place' was *cēping*, and it is the origin of Chipping as prefixed to Barnet Hrt, Sodbury and Campden Gl, Norton O, and Ongar Ess. Chipping La is from the same word; and 'The Chipping' in Tetbury and Wotton-under-Edge were also market-places. In the place-names Chipley D (*lēah*), Chipstead K, Sr (*stede*) and Kepwick YN (*wīc*), we have a related word *cēap*, 'merchandise, a market'. In Newbury, Sherborne, Bath, London and Coventry there are street-names derived from this word, such as Cheap Street and Cheapside, where markets were held.

The southern word 'street' is often replaced in the North by 'Gate', from ON *gata*, 'a way, path or street', which is not to be confused with OE *geat*, 'an opening, gap or gate'. As against Carter Lane Lo, we have Carter Gate, Nottingham, both meaning 'street of the carters'; but many towns were walled for their defence and streets leading directly to gateways in the walls were usually named from the gates. For example, Ludgate (Hill) Lo was a postern-gate (OE *ludgeat*) in the city ramparts and Aldersgate (Street) was 'the gate of one *Ealdred*'. In Colchester, St Botolph's Gate was near the priory of that name and The Head

Gate (ie 'the chief') gave on to the London road. Coventry and Gloucester, among other cities, have interesting gate-names. In York, Bootham Bar, Micklegate Bar, Monk Bar and Walmgate Bar refer to the gates (bars) which, when closed, blocked the stone archways. 'Bar', from Old French *barre*, was a gate-fastening. Bootham meant 'at the booths', from the Old West Scandinavian dative plural *búðum*; for here were situated the stalls of a weekly market. In Micklegate we have OE *mycel*, 'great' and ON *gata*, 'street', the equivalent of 'High Street' in a southern town; and the entrance through the city walls took its name from the street and not from the gateway. Similarly, Monkgate meant 'the monks' (OE *munuc*) street' and Walmgate was probably '*Walba*'s street'. On the other hand, Stonegate, which is not related topographically to any of the city gates, was 'the stone (ON *steinn*)-paved street'. Burgate, Canterbury was simply 'city (*burh*)-gate', but the minor names Burgate Ha, Sf, Sr refer to the entrances to fortified manor-houses (*burh*).

The main medieval entrance through the ramparts of Southampton, the Bargate, has the same Old French *barre* as first element and the suffix '-gate' here does refer to the fortified gateway. West Barrs, Chesterfield were the western barriers to the New Market, which came into existence soon after 1204. West, North and South Bar, which converge on the probable site of Banbury Cross, where they make a junction with the High Street, similarly referred to a barrier at the principal entrance to the town.

A more elaborately defended gateway was a barbican (OF *barbacane*) and the London street of that name was probably so called from an outer part of the fortification of Aldersgate. There is a Barbican in Barnstaple and there was formerly one in Exeter. The main stronghold of a town, the castle, existed in many of our towns and cities, including some from which all trace of it has long since disappeared; but Castle Streets abound, or Castlegate (eg Newark upon Trent) in the North. Its court-yard (OF *baille*) is probably referred to in Bailey St, Oswestry, in the (North and South) Bailey at Durham, in The Bailey, Skipton and in the Baile, York. Castle Street (and Mount Street, for that matter) in Bethnal Green Lo is unusual in that it probably commemorates a fort built by the parliamentary army in 1643.

As archery practice was compulsory for the citizens, shooting-butts, long mounds of earth or stones, turved over, were provided immediately behind the marks or targets. The Butts, Brentford, Warwick, Bridlington, Beverley and elsewhere are on the sites of these practice-grounds or are the names of streets leading to them. Another popular pastime was bull-baiting; and the Bull-rings at Birmingham, Beverley, Wakefield and Ludlow and so on, were the venues for this so-called 'sport'. Bulls or other domestic animals that had strayed were committed to the Pin-fold or Pound (p 80). There is a Pinfold Street in Birmingham and Pound Lane, Road or Street in Canterbury, Isleworth and Warminster.

The water supply for both beasts and men was obtained from conduits (eg Conduit Street, Westminster, Stamford and King's Lynn), which were, in their simplest form, artificial channels; or it was taken from pumps (eg Aldgate Pump, Lo). This latter source of water existed as a conduit in Stow's time in the late sixteenth century. He mentions it among a dozen others in the city. Cisterns were provided for convenience of drawing the water and, where natural springs came to the surface, a stone-lined basin, rather than a lead cistern, might be installed. Stan-well Street, Colchester implies this; and Stockwell Lane, Hedon (YE) and Stockwell Gate, Mansfield were springs lined with tree-stumps rather than stone; or more probably they were sur-rounded by stumps to prevent animals fouling the water. Keld-gate, Beverley has ON *kelda*, 'a spring', as first element. It would be equivalent to Spring Street in the south.

It is to be expected that many streets were named from im-portant buildings in them or at the far ends of them. Church Street or Kirkgate is one of the commonest of such names. Minster Street, Abbey Lane, Priory Street, Mill Lane or Wind-mill Road will be found with minor variations all over England. Less common and less obvious is Spittle Road, Lewes, Spital

Hill, Retford or Spitalfields Lo. These names represent a shortened form of OF *hospitale*, usually designating a refuge for the poor or sick, but sometimes a house of the crusading order of The Knights Hospitaller. A somewhat later but similar institution was the Almshouse (eg Almshouse Lane, Wakefield), Poorhouse (Poorhouse Hill, Arundel), Infirmary or Workhouse, which are occasionally included among street-names; but perhaps the commonest of this type is Union Street, wherein was situated the workhouse of a Poor Law union, administered by a combination of parishes under one board of guardians. Several of these names date only from the nineteenth century, but much earlier was the Pesthouse (eg Pesthouse Lane, Watford), which was for those sick of the plague, and equivalent to the modern isolation hospital.

A grimmer sort of isolation was experienced by some of the inhabitants of Clink Street, Southwark, for the street took its name from a prison, as did Counter Court, site of a debtors' prison; and Marshalsea Road was the site of what became the Surrey County Gaol for felons, made infamous by Dickens in *Little Dorrit*. All three of these were in the Borough, just across London Bridge from the city. Gaol Street, Hereford, was the site of the county gaol for Herefordshire. A less formidable incarceration was to be had in the village lock-up, as in Cage Row, Hornchurch, to take but one of several surviving instances of such a name.

As in most respects the towns were merely overgrown villages, with for example, Cambridge having a population of only about 2,250 in AD 1279, the buildings of town and country were little differentiated, apart from the shops and halls of the town gilds. OE *bōðl*, *bōtl* or *bold*, the latter with metathesis, are mainly found in the North and Midlands, with only a few in the South. Bold La, Sa, Bootle Cu, La and Buddle Ha, So, Wt, all meaning simply 'building(s)', are from the uncompounded forms; Newbottle(s) Bk, Du, Nt and Newbold, a common name in the North, are combined with OE *nīwe*. A *bōðltun* was 'an enclosure with buildings' and gives Bolton Cu, La, Nb, We, Yks.

OE *cot*, 'a cottage, a shed', could also be used of a fox's earth, as in the many Foscotes and -cotts, Foxcotes and Foxcotts. Charlcott(e) Ha, Sa and Charl(e)cote W, Wa were 'cottages inhabited by free peasants', then known as 'churls (*ceorl*)' and Prescot(t) Gl, La, O, were small parsonages, the name having as first element *prēost*, 'priest'. Didcot Brk was occupied by one *Dudda*. A shed for storing salt (OE *salt*) is implied in names such as Salcote, Salcott Ess and the common place-name Draycot(t) was a shelter for drays (*dræg*). (See p 65.) In Caldicote He, Caldecote Bd, Bk, Ca, Ch, Hrt, Hu, Nf, Nth, Wa, Caldecott Nth, Ru and Coldcoats La, Nb we have a literal meaning of 'cold (OE *cald*) cottage(s)', though the likely meaning in actual usage was no doubt 'a shelter for travellers', similar to a Coldharbour (p 120). Woodcote Ha, O, Sa, Sr, Wa and Woodcott Ch, Ha were either 'wooden', as opposed to construction in wattle and daub or in rammed earth, or they were situated in or near a wood (*wudu*). In the simple form, there are Coat(e), a frequent name, and Cote Cu, Gl, O, So, Sx. Cot(t)on, another common name, Co(a)tham Du, Nt, So, YN and Cottam Nt, YE are all from *cotum*, the dative plural, meaning 'at the cottages'.

A *būr* was much the same thing, 'cottage or dwelling', and in its modern form appears as Bowers Ess, K, So, Sx or Bures Ess. The compound *būrcot*, with the same meanings, gives Burcot(t) Bk, He, Sa, So. And another kind of humble dwelling was denoted by '(*ge-*)*set*, 'dwelling, stable, fold'. Hethersett Nf has *hæddre*, 'heather' as first element and could have had either the first or the third of the meanings for (*ge-*)*set*. Ossett YW is similarly doubtful; it has the personal name *Osla*. And the original meaning of the first syllable of Betteshanger K and Buildwas Sa, OE (*ge-*)*bytlu* or (*ge-*)*byldu*, is somewhat uncertain also. This word is a mutated form of *bōðl* etc, meaning 'building or house' and it is, of course, related to the modern word 'build-ing'. Betteshanger was 'a building near a hanging wood (*hangra*) and Buildwas 'a building near a swamp (*wæsse*). The ON verb *byggja*, 'to build', gave Middle English the verb *big* and the noun *bigging*, 'a building an outhouse', which is common in minor names such

104

as Biggin(s) Bk, C, Nb, Nt, Sr, YW and Newbiggin Cu, Nb, We, YN. The former is found also as Biggin (Lane), Hitchin and the latter, in variant forms, as Newbiggin (Street etc) in Beverley, Richmond YW, New Malton and York itself.

But a still commoner term was OE *hūs*, ON *hús*, 'house'. It, too, could be used of a building other than a dwelling, as in Salthouse La, Nf, where salt was boiled or stored, or in the common words 'bakehouse' and 'washhouse'. Stonehouse Gl was presumably built of stone (*stān*) and Woodhouse Lei, YW of timber (*wudu*) or it was near a wood. In Newsham La, YN we have a dative plural 'at the new houses'.

A humbler kind of building was a shed (OE *scydd*). This word appears in no major names, but is the second element of the curious Bowshots (Farm) Sx, in which it is compounded with *burh*, 'a fortress', and of Gunshot (Common) Sx, with the personal name *Guma*. A cowshed (OE *scypen*), sometimes still called 'a shippon or shippen' in dialect, occurs in the same forms, Shippen YW, Shippon Brk, as place-names. This word is not related to *scēap*, 'sheep', but to *gesceap*, 'a creation', which gives us our word 'shape', and to OE *sc(e)oppa*, 'shop, booth'. A pigsty (OE *hlōse*) was the original meaning of Loose K and of the first element of Loosley Brk and Losely Sr, which were 'sties in or near a wood or clearing (*lēah*)'. Our word 'sty' was OE *stīg*, which occurs as the ending of Housty and Houxty Nb. The first syllable of these names was OE *hogg*, 'a hog'. The man in charge of the sties was a 'steward'. OE *stīg-weard*, whose office later became exalted to that of a butler or major-domo. The royal house of Scotland and England, the Stuarts, probably derives its family name from this compound word.

More distinctly of the town is The Shambles, the butchers' quarter, which took its name from their benches or stalls (OE *sc(e)amol*). Besides the famous street of this name in York, there were other towns with the same street-name, notably Chippenham and Chesterfield. In some other towns we have, instead, Butcher(s) Row (eg Bristol, Exeter, Salisbury, and Coventry), the term 'Row' (of houses), OE *rāw*, being a common town name.

105

A rat-infested stretch of buildings was sometimes referred to as Rotten Row (OF *raton*) as for example in Lewes and Lichfield. There was a Long Row in Nottingham, an Ironmonger Row in Coventry and Gloucester. Budge Row Lo, a fur mart, was named from OF *bouchet*, 'a kid', presumably because kid-skins were on sale there; and in London again, there is Paternoster Row where rosaries were made and sold. In Ashdown Forest is Forest Row Sx, which must have taken its name from a row of cottages fronting a track, the precursor of the present small town.

Barns were both rural and urban and the *bere-ærn*, 'barley-building', gives its name to Barn(e)s Nb, Sr etc. In the north, ON *hlaða* was more commonly used than *bere-ærn*; Laithes Cu, in the nominative plural and Laytham YW in the dative plural, are uncompounded. Silloth Cu was a 'barn by the sea (OE *sæ*)'.

Already several occupation-names have been mentioned in earlier pages and there are more to be seen on the street name-plates of our towns. Fisher Street, Lewes, Fishergate Ripon, Nottingham and York, Fisher Row, Oxford and Fish Row, Salisbury and many more like them, disused or still existing, indicate the importance of fish, especially dried stock-fish, in the medieval diet. With the fastest transport limited to the pace of pack animals shuffling along unmetalled tracks, fresh fish, except from freshwater fishponds, was unknown away from the coast; and only the wealthy laymen and greater churchmen had fishponds. Yet for at least half the year there was little fresh butcher's meat to be had; and even in summer when it was available for those who could afford it, there were fasts on Fridays. So dried fish and salted flesh were in much demand. Salters Lane, Hastings, Salter Street, Berkeley and Saltergate, Chesterfield represent some of the many local concentrations of men of this trade. And meat that would have been too high to be palatable could be flavoured with spices, hence Spiceal Street, Birmingham, Pepper Lane, Coventry and Pepper Street, Nottingham. Spicer Street, St Albans refers to the merchant and not to his wares.

The various stages of cloth manufacture are also represented. Walker Lane, Derby, was the street of the cloth-dressers or fullers; Walkergate, Beverley is another northern instance. The tenters, who stretched the cloth on a frame with hooks (we still say 'to be on tenter-hooks'), occupied Tenters Close, Coventry and The Drapery, Northampton was a place where cloth was made up.

Fuel could not be had for the gathering in a town and wood had to be brought into it for sale to householders. Wood Street, London, Kingston, Walthamstow and Stratford-upon-Avon were places where it could be bought, although in some instances the name may mean 'street leading to a wood' or even 'street of wooden buildings'.

Some of the many Gold Streets (eg Wellingborough, Kettering, Saffron Walden), were named from goldsmiths and some of the many Silver Streets (eg Wells So, Bedford, Cambridge and Doncaster) may have housed the silversmiths. They were always the more numerous of the two kinds of craftsmen. The ironsmiths were the commonest of all metal-workers and an important element of every community and their trade gives one of the most frequent street-names, Smith Street (eg Exeter, Warwick and Dartmouth).

The rural quality of medieval towns is well illustrated by the frequency of streets named from farm animals. The very common Sheep Street, the less common Lamb Street (Bristol, though this may be named from an inn), Cow Lane or Street (Northampton, Nottingham) and Goose, Duck and Hog Lanes in various towns, speak of animals that were usually to be seen in them. However, the Sheep Streets at Stow-on-the-Wold and Cirencester and possibly at Devizes, too, were remarkable for the great flocks driven through them to the famous sheep fairs. The other farm animals just mentioned were probably permanent residents in the streets named from them.

The names such as Westfield (Wakefield), Eastfield (Peterborough), Northfield Road or Lane (as at Acton Mx) and Southfield Lane (eg Suffield Road, High Wycombe, with the same origin), are surviving tokens of the open fields on which these towns depended for farm produce. East, West, North and South Streets or Lanes, of course, occur very frequently, but they are usually within the ancient limits of the town.

Quite often streets are named from the places to which they led. The frequent Moor Lane (eg Lancaster) was the route to part of the common pasture on 'a moor. Mill Lane or Street is equally frequent; in Hitchin it is Portmill Lane, which led to *the* town (OE *port*) mill. Park Street, Lane etc usually led out of a town and did not, as in Westminster Park Lane, run beside the park from which it took its name. And Tothill or Toothill Street etc would normally have led to a look-out mound outside the town, though one would have thought that a church tower, or similar vantage point on a building within the walls, would have been preferred. At any rate, Toothill Lane and Road are to be found in Mansfield and Loughborough and a Tothill Street in Westminster. The last-named must have been a man-made mound, possibly an ancient barrow referred to at this point in an Anglo-Saxon charter. More distant destinations are implied in the common type of name exemplified by The Old Kent Road, Bermondsey, by London Road, Tring (and scores of other London Roads in southern towns), Edgbaston Street, Birmingham, Banbury Road, Warwick and so on.

Many towns grew up at important river-crossings and their streets make reference to the river. A Bridge Street is to be found in most towns; it is Briggate in Leeds. Many Thames-valley towns have a Thames Street and those along the Severn are named accordingly (eg Gloucester and Newnham). Ferry Street, Lambeth and Horseferry Road, Westminster are typical of many such names. Brook Street and Water Lane (eg Shrewsbury and Saffron Walden) usually lead down to water. Quay Street, Bristol and Lymington and Key Street, Ipswich, run beside it and included the town wharves. Heath Street, Barking had the same meaning, for it is derived from OE *hȳð*. The Strand, London, Barnstaple and Sandwich, were riverside ways; Bankside, Southwark is self-explanatory. Eastover, Bridgwater and Southover, Lewes and Wells (So) have as second element *ōfer*, 'a river-bank'. The common Marsh Lane or Street probably led to the riverside, too, and sometimes the marsh was crossed by an artificial embankment, or causeway, as at Banbury and Chippenham.

Slough Lane, Brinkworth was probably a notoriously muddy one, as few towns ways were paved and into them was cast household and shop refuse, causing them not only to squelch but to stink. When we conjure up idealistic pictures of half-timbered medieval towns, we should remember how noisome and pestilential they really were.

Many streets were named from former residents in them. Trig Lane in the City of London took its name from a family of local importance in the fourteenth century. Bennetts Hill, Birmingham is from a sixteenth-century resident and Mepsale's Corner, Ely from one of a century earlier. And there are many scores of them altogether in our towns. But somewhat different are the Lordship Lanes in Tottenham, Stoke Newington and Dulwich, all in greater London, which refer to the lord of the manor. From the other end of the social scale comes the northern street-name, Bondgate, especially frequent in Yorkshire, which is derived from ON *bondi*, 'an unfree tenant'.

Many streets were named from churches. Botolph Lane, London, was called after the vanished church of St Botolph by Billingsgate, one of eighty-four destroyed in the Great Fire of 1666. Just across the Thames, Tooley Street, Southwark, was known to John Stow as St Olave's Street from the local parish church. The final 't' of the word 'Saint' was wrongly attached to 'Olave' and the second syllable weakened to '-ey'. In Bradford-on-Avon there was a *Tuley Streete* in the seventeenth century, so called from a chapel of St Olave. By a wrongful association of ideas the name became Woolley Street because it does, in fact, lead to Woolley ('the wolves' wood'). St Martin's Lane, Lewes and Pancras Lane, Exeter are but two of the numerous instances of this kind. The loss of 'Saint' from the Exeter example is not uncommon in this kind of street-name. But those such as Angel

Lane, Northampton are from inns. Again, they are very numerous, though few are so well known as White Hart Lane, Tottenham, which was already so called in 1600. Swan Lane, Guildford and Coventry; Sun Street, Waltham Holy Cross and Hitchin; and Chequers Street, St Alban's will suffice as instances.

The designations of the various kinds of thoroughfare are in themselves of some interest. The word 'lane' is from OE *lane* or *lanu* and referred, as now, to minor routes in town or country; yet few country lanes are recorded as such in medieval documents, though they may well have been named by the peasants. The word 'way', which occurs very commonly in town and country names, is derived from OE *weg*, 'a way, a path'. It was used of the great Roman road, originally a frontier line from Seaton D to Lincoln, the Fosse Way. 'Fosse' is either a direct borrowing from Latin *fossa*, 'a ditch' or was borrowed from an Old British word which itself was a loan from Latin. The term 'fosse' was given to the Roman road because of the ditches which flanked its sides. These ditches provided the material for the *agger*, the mound upon which the road-metalling was placed. The ditches would have seemed the more prominent because of the mound between them. The pre-Roman route from The Wash, along the Chiltern scarp to the Goring Gap on the Thames, was called the Icknield Way, but the origin and meaning of the descriptive word are unknown.

A common name, Broadway Hu, So, Sr, W, Wo, which is obvious in meaning, was given to settlements established beside such routes, as well as to wide town streets (eg Bristol, Bradford). This name continues to be given where it is appropriate: Hammersmith Broadway Lo is not recorded before 1813 and Tolworth Broadway Sr was constructed and named in the nineteen-thirties. But a much older name is Holloway D, Lo, W etc, which was given to roads that had been worn down until they became hollow (OE *hol*) tracks. The absence of metalling hastened the process, especially on slopes. Stanway (OE *stān*, 'paved') Ess, Gl, He, Sa had an artificial hard surface at the time of naming and was usually Roman in origin, but a Ridgeway Brk, K, O W, etc, is normally an unmetalled track following ridges (OE *hrycg*) across country, sometimes having the appearance of a Whiteway D, Do, Gl where it cut into chalk or limestone. Before the days of metalled roads, the ridgeways provided dry routes above the sloughs and marshes of the valleys, passable even in winter when the lowland tracks were unfit for use. In some parts of the country, this state of affairs persisted even into the nineteenth century.

The Saltways Gl, He, Sa converged on the salt-producing neighbourhood of Droitwich Wo, which was called Saltwich in a charter purporting to be a copy of one dating back to AD 717. The later name seems to have meant 'buildings (*wīc*) in a dirty (OE *drit*) place', the dirt perhaps being the industrial waste from salt-boiling. If any of these routes, ridgeways, whiteways or saltways, passed through or near a market-town (OE *port*), it might be termed The Portway C, D, Db, O, Wo.

The French verb *aller*, in its past participle (OF *alee*) is the source of our word 'alley', but Fenkle or Finkle, a common street-name of the north (eg Carlisle, Oakham, Alnwick, Hull and eight or nine more) is less easily explained. There was a Middle English *fenkel*, meaning 'a corner or bend', and although some Fenkle Streets are now straight, it is known that they were not so formerly. But the origin of this word *fenkel* is somewhat doubtful, although there is a Germanic root which is represented by Danish *vinkel* and by OE *wincel*, 'a corner', which is found in our place-names. The 'f' of *fenkel* is probably a relic of its borrowing into English from Low German in the Middle Ages.

The word 'street' was borrowed into English while the tribes were still in their continental homelands. It is from Latin (*via*) *strāta*, 'a way spread (with metalling)'. '*Strata*' is the past participle of the Latin verb *sternere*, 'to spread (flat), to pave (a road)'. In early Anglo-Saxon times, after the settlement in Britain, *strǣt* was used of a Roman road (see Stratton, Stretton, p 99), but in the late Old English it came to be used of a road in a town, presumably because it was paved or metalled. The modern sense of the word 'road' is not, however, found before Shakespeare's day, at any rate in literature. OE *rād*, denoted 'the act of riding' and perhaps also 'suitable for riding' and is related to the OE verb *rīdan*, 'to ride'. It is interesting that *rād* gives us both 'road' and 'raid', the latter word implying an attack made after riding.

With the expansion of the towns in the fifteenth and following centuries, New Street (eg Birmingham) was an obvious name to give, but the much greater urban expansion of the nineteenth-century seems to have exhausted the possibilities of naming streets by the older principles, and 'artificial' naming was resorted to. Liverpool seems to have drawn heavily on London in its borrowing of Marylebone, Wapping, Islington, Whitechapel and Kensington. It also has Kingsway, Hatton Garden, Cheapside, Soho Street, Mount Pleasant and Cable Street, though a few of these names are possibly true local products. Bond Street occurs in northern towns more often than one would expect as a derivative from ON *bondi*; and it may sometimes have been adopted for fashionable shopping streets aping the London thoroughfare. Commercial Road or Street, which may be found almost anywhere, was probably a more original naming.

In the first half of the nineteenth century it was usual to name streets after such battles as Trafalgar (eg Bradford, Gravesend) or Waterloo (Wolverhampton, Bedford) or after Wellington and Nelson; and in the middle of the century, the battles of the Crimea, Inkerman and Alma provided street-names. The Queen, too, was commemorated in many a Victoria Street or Road and so were her statesmen, especially Palmerston, Disraeli, and Gladstone. Where battle-names were used, it is usually possible to date the building of a street of houses to within a year or two of the event.

The new suburbs of London which were built in the eighteenth century and later had some older naming material at hand. Where roads were built on the sites of former country seats, their names or those of the owners were often perpetuated. Thus arose Ashburnham Road and Beaufort Street, Chelsea; similarly Burlington Road and Devonshire Road, Chiswick—and from the Duke of Devonshire's other estates came the names of Bolton and Hartington Roads, also in Chiswick. In Fulham, Talgarth Road and neighbouring streets were called after the Breconshire estates of the Gunters, whose family name was included in Gunterstone Road. Russell Square, Bedford Square, Woburn Square and other street-names in Holborn are taken from the family name, the titles and the estates of the Dukes of Bedford. This new suburb of London was laid out in about 1775. Compton Terrace, Marquess Road and Northampton Park, Islington are names similarly referring to the Marquess of Northampton. Pentonville took its name from Henry Penton, who developed his estate in 1773. In Kensington, Barkston and Bramham Gardens, with Wetherby Road, were so called from places in the West Riding near the speculative builder's home. The same is true of Chepstow Villas, Ledbury Road and so on, which were near the Hereford home of another mid-nineteenth century builder. Onslow Square and Cranley Gardens are built on land once owned by the Earl of Onslow, whose eldest son bore the title Viscount Cranley. Finally, Edwardes Square, also in Kensington, was built about 1804 on land held by the Pembrokeshire family of Edwardes—hence streets and squares named from Nevern, Pembroke, Penywern and so on.

Not infrequently, streets were called after great men who had lived locally. Carlyle Square, Chelsea, Hogarth Lane, Chiswick and Sloane Square with Hans Place, are but a few London instances of this practice. Speculative builders, who had not owned the land on which they built, are commemorated in Newton Street, Holborn (1629), Allen Street, Kensington (1820) and Wright's Lane, Kensington (*circa* 1774). And there are many more of this kind both in London and in the provinces.

CHAPTER 7

Localised Words

During the main period of place-name formation in Anglo-Saxon times, communications in England were little, if at all, better than they had been in later prehistoric times. This tended to isolate communities one from another, a tendency strengthened by the division of the country into a number of relatively small princedoms. As the language then, as now, was changing and developing, imperceptibly in any one generation, the changes (which were, of course, quite involuntary), would not have been simultaneous or precisely similar everywhere, so that some aspects of the spoken language would have changed faster in one region than in another. As a result, there was more regional diversity in the speech of medieval people than there had been in, say, the seventh century. The language had been changing even before the migrations of the English tribes to Britain and it has gone on changing steadily ever since. No one who has studied a page of Chaucer in the original late fourteenth-century English can have any doubt of how extensive the changes have been during the last five hundred years; and Chaucer was writing in the East Midland dialect which is ancestral to modern standard English. The West Midland poem, 'Sir Gawayne and the Green Knight', is far more remote from us in vocabulary, grammar and syntax than Chaucer's verse, yet although 'Sir Gawayne' was written only about a generation before his time, the language of the two poems shows striking dialectal differences.

Here we are concerned only with vocabulary and especially

114

with that peculiar to certain regions. But only a few of the many local words can be considered and particularly those that are not infrequent in the place-names of a region; the rarer ones are ignored.

The superimposition of Scandinavian habits of speech on the Anglian dialects of the North and East is a main cause of the broad distinction between the place-names of the Danelaw on the one hand and of those regions to the south and west of it which were not settled by the Danes or Norwegians. Yet even within the Danelaw, especially in the North-West where the Norwegian–Irish had settled, there were localised habits of naming places, and it is these that claim attention first.

In Norway, as in Switzerland and some other mountainous countries of Europe, the whole rhythm of life was based on transhumance, the migration of flocks and herds from the valleys, where they wintered, progressively up the Alpine slopes as far as pasture extended. On their migration up and down again, temporary shelters were built for the use of the cowherds and shepherds. The Cumbrian and Pennine mountains provided similar conditions, even though the altitudes were less. And there are several words which were commonly used there which meant 'temporary shelter or shieling' and, by an extension of meaning 'hill or summer pasture'.

The first of these, ON *erg*, was a loan-word from Irish. On the modern map it takes such forms as Arrowe Ch, in the dative singular, and Argam, Arram YE, Arkholme La, in the dative plural. In compounds it appears as Birker Cu, with ON *birki*, 'birch-tree'; Medlar La, with OE *middel*; Winder La, We, with OE *wind*, 'windy'; or it may be prefixed by an Old Irish personal name, as in Coldman Hargos YN (*Colman*) or by an ON name, as in Mansergh We (*Man*). Almost identical in meaning, as far as we can tell, was ON *sǽtr*, which again is largely limited to the north-western mountainous regions. Seatoller Cu was 'the shieling by the alders (OE *alor*); Forcett YN was by a waterfall (ON *fors*) and Hawkshead La was associated with a certain *Haukr*. Often, the modern form of *sǽtr* is—'-side' when it is a

115

final syllable, as in Greenside, with *grene*, 'green', or Gunnerside YN, with the personal name *Gunnar*.

The word *skáli*, from West Scandinavian, the language of the territory now called Norway, meant 'a temporary hut'. It is found mainly in the same English regions as *erg* and *sætr*, but it occurs also on the eastern side of England. The place-names Scales Cu, La, YN and Scholes La, YW are variant developments of this word uncompounded. Gatesgill Cu, with ON *geit*, 'a goat', and Winscales, Winskill Cu, with *wind*, are instances of its use in compounds. Its cognate, OE *scēla*, is found mainly in Northumberland and Durham. North and South Shields are derived from the simple form of the word; Shelley Nb, with *lēah*, 'a clearing' exemplifies its use in a compound.

A distinctively northern use of the word 'bank' (Old Danish *banke*) was used to describe the slope of a hill. This connotation of the word is almost unknown in the south. The word is found frequently in medieval and later field-names, as in Bank(s), Bankend, Yew Bank etc Cu, and Bank Head Db, Nb. Firbank We and Bank Newton YW are instances from among major names. 'Bank' in this sense is still a part of the living vocabulary of many people of the north of England. It came to be used of the artificial ridge of earth alongside a river, an '(em-)bank-(-ment)' and to describe, with an extension of meaning, the slopes above a river, forming its valley; and it is now used, of course, of the flat margins of a river, lake or pond. The cognate OE *benc*, 'bench', possibly had an extended meaning 'shelf, bank', and certainly there is confusion between this word and *banke*. Kate's Bank W and Ninebanks Nb (OE *nigon*. 'nine') are in fact from *benc*.

In one of its meanings, 'a conical hill', OE *pīc* is very frequent in the minor names of the north, though it does occur sporadically elsewhere. Red Pike and Stone Pike Cu, Rivington Pike La, the Langdale Pikes We, including Pike o' Stickle (with OE *sticol*, 'a steep place'), Pigdon Nb (with *dūn*, 'hill'), Pickup Bank La (*pīc* + OE *copp*, 'hill-top' + *banke*, 'hill-slope'), Pickhill Ess and Pick Hill K are instances illustrating the variety of its uses;

116

but it could also mean the fish called 'pike' as in Pickburn YW (OE *burna*, 'a stream') and Pickmere Ch (OE *mere*, 'a pool'); and it had a third meaning, 'a prickle', as in Pickthorn Sa. Moreover, there was an OE personal name *Pīca*, which is the first element in names such as Pickworth L, Ru (*worð*, 'an enclosure') and Picton Ch, YN (*tūn*, 'a farm').

OE *clōh*, 'a ravine or dell' survives in North Country dialect as 'clough'. In place-names it is the first syllable of Clotton Ch, Cloughton YW (both with *tūn*) and the final syllable in Catcleugh Nb (with OE *catte*, 'a she-cat', probably the native wild cat), and Deadwin Clough La, of which the first word was *dēad cwene*, 'a dead woman', no doubt referring to the finding of a corpse in the ravine. A shallower valley, Old West Scandinavian *slakki*, is the origin of Slack La, YW, Hazelslack We (with ON *hesli*, 'hazel'), and Nettleslack La (OE *netele*, 'nettle'). And in the bottom of such a valley, or beside a stream, there might well be a *marr*, an ON term for 'a fen or marsh'. It was often confused with its cognate, OE *mere*, 'a pool', as in Eelmere YE (OE *āl*, 'eel') or Whitwood Mere (OE *hwīt*, 'white' + *wudu*); but the normal development of the word is found in Marfleet YE (with OE *flēot*, 'estuary', ie The Humber) and in Marton YN; but most of the other Martons eg Ch, La, L, W, YE, YW are from OE *meretūn*, 'farm by the pool' (p 68). (The) Marr(s) YE, YW show the development of OM *marr* in uncompounded place-names.

Another word for 'a marshy place' (or 'a spring') was ON *kelda*, a cognate of OE *celde*, 'a spring' (see p 63). The alternative meanings of the ON term arose quite naturally, for a spring often produces a marsh where it rises. In Kellet La and Kelleth We, it is combined with OE *hlið*, 'a hill-side'; in Calkeld La, Cawkeld YE, Cawkhill YW and Cold Keld YN it has the meaning 'cold (OE *cald*) spring'; and Threlkeld Cu was the 'serfs' (ON *þræll*) spring'). Another topographical term, ON *skógr*, 'a wood or shaw (OE *sceaga* is a cognate) gives modern names such as Scaws, Sceugh, Schoose Cu; and in compounds with tree-names Aiskew YN (ON *eik*, 'oak'), Ellershaw Cu (ON *elri*, 'alder') and Thrunscoe L (ON *þyrnir*, 'thorn-bush'); and Briscoe YN has ON *birki*,

117

'birch', yet Briscoe Cu has *Brettas* as first element, the whole place-name having the meaning 'Britons' wood'.

Yet another Scandinavian word, but one lacking cognates in the other German languages is ON *topt*, Old Danish *toft*. In England it is largely absent from the north-western shires where the Irish-Norwegian settlement introduced other usages. It is to be regarded as distinctively Danish rather than Norwegian in its origin. Its meaning in England was 'the plot of ground on which a building stands' and its widespread use in the legal phrase 'toft and croft' may have caused it to spread southwards, for it occurs in Bedfordshire, Buckinghamshire and Essex, though, in any case, the northern half of Bedfordshire and a northern strip of Buckinghamshire were in the Danelaw. Standing alone, this word is a common place-name: Toft C, Hu, L, Nb, Nf, Sf, Wa, YW, YE. It is the second element in many compounds such as Langtoft L, YE (OE *lang*, 'long'), Saintoft(s) YE, YN, 'a toft cleared by burning (OE *senget*)' and Willitoft YE (OE *wilig*, 'willow'). It is very common also with a personal name prefixed, as, for instance, Lowestoft Sf (*Hloðver*) and Wibtoft L (*Vibbe*, an Old Swedish personal name). Furthermore, the term *toft* is found in large numbers of northern and midland field-names.

The West Midlands had fewer distinctive place-name elements. *Worðign*, 'an enclosure', is the most important. It interchanges sometimes with *worð* and *worðig*, for all have the same meaning. The term *worðign* is distributed over a region comprising the northern half of Gloucestershire, throughout Worcestershire, Staffordshire, Cheshire and Lancashire, but it is especially frequent in Herefordshire and Shropshire. Worthin, Sa (uncompounded), Chickward He (OE *cicen*, 'chicken'), Faldingworth La (apparently 'enclosure by the fold (OE *fald*)', Northenden Ch (*norð*), are varied instances; with river-names we have Leintwardine (River Lent), and Lugwardine (River Lugg), both He. It must be added that a few examples are found in Devon: Bradworthy (*brād*, 'broad'), and Badgworthy ('*Bacga*'s enclosure'); but in this county, *worðig* is the commonest form of the three, in so far as their early forms are distinguishable. Devonshire names in *worð* and *worðig* total over 180; there is possibly a dozen in *worðign* in that county. *Worð* is found in all southern and midland counties, in southern Lancashire, the south of the West Riding, in Northumberland and in Durham. There is only one instance in the North Riding, but none in the East Riding, Cumberland or Westmorland. The blank area extends from both sides of the Humber estuary north-westwards to Solway Firth.

One of the commonest of all words in place-name compounds is *wella*, 'a well, spring or stream'. This is the Anglian and Kentish form, as in Greetwell L (OE *grēot*, 'gravel') or Chalkwell K (OE *cealc*, 'chalk'). There are variant forms in West Saxon: *wi(e)lla, wielle, wyll(a)*, and *wylle*, which in the southwestern shires occasionally survives as '-will' in names like Halwill and Will D. Halwill was a 'holy (OE *hālig*) spring' and this name recurs in the same county as Halwell. The form 'well' is the one that became established in standard English; it was the one normal in the East Midlands, whose dialect eventually became standard. Even in late Anglo-Saxon times, '-well' was beginning to displace the local forms—hence Halwell D. Elsewhere, this same place-name occurs as Haliwell Mx, Halliwell La, Hallwell Co and, in many counties, as Holy Well or Holywell.

The West Saxon forms *wylle* and *wyll(a)* would normally have become *wull* in Middle English and the names Wool, and Woolcombe Do, 'spring in a combe (OE *cumb*)', are survivals of this sound development. In Mercia, however, especially in Wo, He, Sa, St, Db, Ch, south Lancs, and a few neighbouring areas, *wælla* and *wælle* were the usual local forms; and these became *walle* in Middle English. In names like Wall Sa, Colwall He (OE *cald*, 'cold'), and Crabwall Ch (OE *crabba*, 'a crayfish'), the OE local form has survived into modern English, but in others, such as Bakewell, '*Badeca*'s spring' and Tideswell, '*Tīdi*'s spring', both of them in the Mercian parts of Derbyshire, there was a struggle in Middle English between the Mercian-*walle* and the East Midland -*welle*—a struggle that is to be seen in the documents that record these names; but the -*welle* form triumphed in the end.

The OE term *bold* (p 103) is another predominantly Mercian

119

form of what, in other Anglian regions of the Midlands and North, was *boðl* or *bōtl*, 'a building'. And ME *dingle*, 'a dell', has a distribution similar to that of *bold*. Its use is illustrated by such names as (The) Dingle G, La, Wa, Dingley Nth (*lēah*) and Dinglewell Gl.

We have already seen how frequently *worðign* occurs in the South-West and especially in Devon. OE *land-scearu*, 'a share of land, a landmark, a boundary', has a roughly similar distribution. It was the first element of Lancercombe (*cumb*) and Langsford (*ford*) D and Launcherly So (*lēah*); and it is found as a field-name as far east as Wiltshire, with the modern form 'Landshare'. OE *crundel* is more typical of the south country as a whole, though instances are found as far north as Cambridgeshire and Worcestershire. It had the meaning 'quarry, chalkpit'. Crondall Ha, Crowndale D, Crundale K and Crundall Wo are some instances of the forms to be seen on the modern map.

There are over 300 instances of the minor name Coldharbour in thirty-four shires, mostly in the south. It is derived from OE *c(e)ald herebeorg*, literally 'cold army-shelter', but with the more general connotation of 'a bleak situation', topographically. Very few examples of this name are to be found in early records; indeed, the earliest are of the fourteenth century and the great majority of the seventeenth or later when, as we know from literary sources, the name was in great vogue and was given to farms and houses, some of them newly built. But in origin, the name is old and forms such as *Herberg(en)*, 'shelters, inns', are found on the modern map of Germany. This fact demonstrates that the word and its meaning 'shelter' belong to the common West Germanic vocabulary and that it did not arise only in the English branch of the language. But there is no evidence on the Germanic continent or here that the term was applied to ancient remains, Roman or other, as has sometimes been asserted by antiquaries.

Largely limited to neighbouring areas of Surrey and Hampshire, and with only a few instances as far away as Cumberland and Nottinghamshire, OE *scēat* is more truly a local word in usage than most of those considered earlier. It is related to the verb *scēotan*, 'to shoot', and meant 'a projecting piece of land, an angle of land'. It is most often combined with words for vegetation as in Aldershot Ha (*alor*) or with personal names, as in Oxshott Sr (*Ocga* or *Occa*), which is situated in a projecting corner of the parish of Stoke D'Abernon. Bagshot Sr may also have a personal name *Bacga*, or, perhaps, *bagga*, 'badger' (p 24). Further to the south-east is the region of another localised term, OE *denn*, 'a woodland pasture, a swine pasture', in the ancient forest land of the Weald of Kent and Sussex. Cowden K, Sx (with *cū*, 'cow'); Tenterden K, 'swine pasture of the men of the Isle of Thanet (*Tenetwaru*)'; Benenden K, '*denn* of *Bionna*'s people (*Bionningas*)'; and Rolvenden K, '*denn* of *Hrōðwulf*'s people (*Hrōðwulfingas*)', exemplify some of its uses in place-names.

Finally, a suffix rather than a word—and one that has several origins, namely -*et(e)* or *ett(e)*. This gives rise to many familiar place-names and associated surnames. The Germanic -*ett(e)* is the commoner of the two, and most often it is added to a tree-name to give the meaning 'a place significant because of what is named', in some instances, and 'a clump of—' in others. For instance, Rushett(s) K, Sr, Sx was 'a place characterised by rushes (OE *rysc*)'; St Ives Ha, 'a clump (or exuberant growth) of ivy (OE *īfett*)'; and besides Birchett(s) Sr, 'a birch-clump' and Chislett K, 'a chestnut copse' (p 31), there are a number of further instances among very rare or very minor place-names. And it will be noticed that these, too, are south-eastern in their distribution, though they are not exclusively so. But the -*ett(e)* which comes from French and has diminutive force, as in 'pullet, fillet, bullet', is less important in place-names though more widely spread in everyday use. Hampnett Gl, Sx was originally the common place-name (*æt*) *hēantūne*, '(at) the high farm' (usually Hampton in its modern form), but by the thirteenth century the French suffix had been added. In Somerset, Cricket (Malherbie and St Thomas) were named from a hill (British *crūc*) and first one and then the other of these place-names had the -*et* suffix added.

CHAPTER 8

Death and Burial

Until fairly recent times, death was a familiar sight to people of all classes. Only a minute proportion of the population ended its days in a hospital, there was a very high rate of infant mortality and violent death was even commoner than it is in the mid-twentieth century. In its many aspects, death afforded one of the themes that entered into the naming of places.

Burials, with their visible evidence on the surface of the ground, gave points of reference in topography, especially by their inclusion in the bounds of estates and parishes. Barrows, under various names, are still very numerous in many parts of England; they were formerly even more common, many having been ploughed out during the last twenty years. The word 'barrow' itself is from OE *beorg*, which could also be used with reference to a natural hill. At Modbury Do the hundred-moot (OE *ge-mōt*) probably met at a barrow; Woodnesborough K may refer to a barrow, rather than a hill, that was associated with the pagan god *Wōden* (pp 148-9); and Thrybergh YW was, or perhaps still is, a group of three (OE *þrī*) tumuli. OE *hlāw* had the same meanings, though it refers more often to a burial mound than does *beorg*. Taplow Bk still has a Saxon barrow in its churchyard from which the precious possessions of *Tæppa* were removed to the British Museum. The Bartlow (Hills) C were overgrown with birch (OE *beorc*) trees and were heaped high over the cremated remains of Belgic aristocrats who died about a century after the Roman conquest but persisted in their customary

122

burial rites. Mutlow Ch had the same meaning as Modbury Do, above. Drakelow Wo was thought to contain a hoard of precious grave-goods guarded by a dragon (OE *draca*) and in Hurdlow (Hartington) Db the treasure (OE *hord*) is specified (p 153).

Throughout the Danelaw, ON *haugr* is the usual term for 'a hill or burial mound'. In Yorkshire, Lincolnshire, Norfolk and Suffolk, it largely displaces the word *hlāw*, and in the North Country as a whole, it is common in minor names. Howe Nf, YE, YN may have either meaning, but there is, in fact, a tumulus near the East Riding place, in Kilburn parish. Galley (Lane) L once ran past a mound surmounted by gallows (ON *galgi*) and Shunner Howe YN was probably a look-out (ON *sjón*) point. Spell Howe YE is a barrow where speech (OE *spell*) occurred and was at one time, no doubt, the meeting-place of a hundred, called in this region, 'a wapentake' (ON *vápnatak*). The name is therefore comparable with Modbury Do and Mutlow Ch, mentioned above.

The less frequent term OE *hær*, which is ultimately related to 'cairn' (British *carn-*), had the meanings, 'a rock, a stone-heap, a burial-mound or cairn'. It is the origin of the first syllable of Harland YN, 'barrow-land', with OE or ON *land*; and many barrows still survive there. In Harome YN and Herne Bd, we have the dative plural of this word *hær*, with the meaning 'at the barrows'. Its cognate, British *carn-* is to be found even less frequently on the map. It lies behind names such as Char Do, Charn Brk and Cerne Do—all originally river-names—and Charnwood and Charnley Lei. Its meaning, 'a heap of stones, a cairn', suggests that it may not always refer to places of burial; but how such a term came to be applied to the rivers it is difficult to say. ON *hreysi* had the same meaning as *carn-* and it explains many of the Raise names of the North-West, such as Raisthwaite La (ON *þveit*), Raise and Dunmaile Raise Cu. This last name may well refer to the cairn in which a tenth-century prince of Strathclyde, *Dunmail*, was interred. Stone Raise YN and Toppin Rays La (OE *topping*, 'hill-top'), are further examples;

and Harras Cu is tautological in that its first syllable was the word OE *hær*, just mentioned, the second being ON *hreysi*, both of which meant 'cairn'.

Burial-places, including barrows, could be referred to as *byrgels*, an OE word, like the next to be considered, related to the verb 'to bury' (OE *byrigan*). It is found mainly in minor names such as Heathens' Burial Corner, Steyning Sx, where 'scores of urns', presumably cinerary urns of the Bronze Age, were said to have been found. A secondary form of this word, OE *brægels*, may be the origin of Brailes Wa, Brailsford Db and Brailsham Sx. OE *byrgen*, with the same meaning, is the source of the first syllable of Burnhill Bk, where a barrow still exists; of Hebburn Du, with *hēa*, 'high'; and Kinsbourne Hrt was 'Cyne's burial-place'. It is in a neighbourhood rich in prehistoric and Roman finds. A third related noun, OE *burgæsn*, seems to be confined to northern counties: Borrans (Hill) and Borrowscale (ON *skáli*, 'a shieling'), both in Cumberland, and Bornesses YN.

It was a custom among some of the first Anglo-Saxon immigrants to cremate their dead on a funeral pyre (OE *ād*). The Node (Condicote) Hrt incorporates the word, though possibly it meant 'an ash-heap' in this context. There is, however, a name Noades Leaze in Cold Ashton Gl where tenth-century boundary points include *þa hæþenan byrigelsas*, 'the heathen burials', which may possibly have been early Saxon. It would be unusual nevertheless, for cremations of this period to be discovered so far to the west. And OE *bēl* could mean 'a funeral pyre' as well as 'a (beacon) fire'. It is a word that occurs in several village-names as well as in those of minor places. Bylaugh and Belaugh Nf, both compounded with *haga*, meaning presumably 'cremation enclosure' and Belgrave Lei, with *grāf*, 'a grove', are in areas where Anglian cremation burials have been discovered. Belton Lei, L (two instances in Lincs), R, Sf are compounded with *tūn*. Cremation almost entirely ceased early in the Anglo-Saxon period and it was contemporary with the older meaning of *tūn*, 'an enclosure'. Probably, then, *tūn* had this connotation in the place-name Belton, which would have meant 'cremation enclosure'. Beltoft and Belwood L are near the Belton L which is in the Isle of Axholme from which no early Anglian remains are yet known. Byley in the parish of Lockington YE has the same origin and meaning as Bylaugh and Belaugh Nf.

There are two Belsteads, 'place of fire', one of which is in the parish of Broomfield Ess. It was in this same parish that a rich grave was discovered of which the excavator said: 'the body had been placed in a stout coffin and burnt as it lay on the ground'. There is a possibility that Belstead acquired its name from this practice. The other Belstead is three miles south-west of Ipswich Sf where, in a pagan cemetery consisting mainly of inhumation burials, there were a few cremated burials. The minor name Beald (Farm) C, near Ely, is also to be derived from *bēl* and a twelfth-century document refers to the place as *Bele super Dedehil*, which indicates that a tradition of burial was associated with the hill.

The famous Jutish cemetery on Chessel Down Wt, was surrounded by an earthwork which may well have been called a *haga*, 'enclosure', though this word does not enter into the place-name Chessell, which probably meant 'coffin (OE *cest*) hill (*hyll*)'. But there were, in fact, a few cremations among the oldest graves and some of the other burials were lined with upright stones, suggesting a rudimentary coffin or cist. Chestham in Henfield Sx may also contain the word *cest*, referring possibly to a Roman or Saxon coffin-burial unearthed in later Saxon times; but the name may be derived from OE *cist*, a shortened form of *cist(en)-bēam*, 'chestnut tree', or from Middle English *cheste*, 'strife', a memory of some long-past dispute over possession of the land there. Chesland W and Chest Wood Ess are both on parish boundaries and were no doubt areas in dispute between neighbouring village communities. The first element of these names very probably goes back to OE *ceast*, which became ME *cheste* or *chyste*. Quarrels of this kind were less likely in Anglo-Saxon times during which productive lands were still encircled by an ever-diminishing band of forest or heathland, not generally worth quarrelling over.

The word *dēad* is not infrequent in minor names, sometimes in towns, but more often in the countryside and it usually refers to a place where someone met a violent death or where ancient human remains were discovered. The phrases *þa hæþenan byrigelsas* and *dedehill*, mentioned above, are instances of this kind of name. Dead Lake D (OE *lacu*, 'stream'), Deadman Croft YW, Deadman's Coppice (1275) Gl, Deedle Hill YE (which is tautological: 'Dead hill [*hyll*] Hill'), and Deadwin Clough La ('dead woman' [OE *cwene*] valley (OE *clōh*)) are rural examples; Dead Lane is to be found in the town of Ware Hrt. If murder (OE *morð*) were suspected, then the place-name might record it, as in Morpeth Nb (OE *pæð*) and Mortgrove Hrt (OE *grāf*, 'grove', 'wood'); and the discovery of a corpse (OE *līc*) is referred to in Lickpit Ha (OE *pytt*), Litchborough Nth (*beorg*, 'hill or barrow'), Lychpole Sx (OE *pōl*, 'pool') and Litchaton D, which meant 'enclosure (*tūn*) for bodies', that is 'a cemetery'. An alternative word for 'corpse', OE *wæl*, occurs in the name Wellesbourne Wa (OE *burna*, 'stream').

The term *bana* ('slayer'), did not imply criminality to the Anglo-Saxons as its modern equivalent does to us. If the slayer acted in self-defence or in execution of the law, he was held to be blameless, and no doubt many a murder committed in a solitary place was justified by the plea of self-defence. Their attitude to killing is illustrated by the fact that many murders could be bought off by payment of a *wergild* to the victim's relations. It varied in amount according to the rank of the slain man. Yet the Laws of King Ine of Wessex (688–694) lay it down that, if a thief were caught in the act, he should die the death (*swelte he deaðe*) or his life could be redeemed by his *wergild*; and the same fate awaited the foreigner who strayed from the track or who was passing through a wood without shouting or sounding his horn. But a penally enslaved Englishman who ran away had no alternative to being hanged. Athelstan's Laws (he reigned 924–939) imposed the death penalty for witchcraft, for the theft of property valued about twelve pence and, in certain circumstances, for disturbance of the peace. But what we term murder was not necessarily punishable by death. The word *bana* was the first element of Bonchurch Wt, of Bannawell D and Banwell So (both with *wella*, 'a spring').

The 'place of execution' (OE *cwealm-stow*) was the meaning of Swamstey (Common) in Clothall parish Hrt; and in the same county are Galley (Lane), parish of Ridge, and Gallows Hill (in both Abbots Langley and Kelshall parishes). And many minor names from OE *galga* or ON *galgi* are to be found all over the country and especially in the North. Galligill Cu (ON *haugr*), Gowbarrow Cu and Gawber YW, both with OE *beorg*, commemorate the setting up of gallows on natural eminences or on burial-mounds, as does Gallowlow Lane (OE *hlāw*) in Brassington Db. Leicester has a Gallowtree Gate, Newcastle upon Tyne a Gallowgate and Warwick, a Gallows Street. An alternative word, *hēafod-stocc*, survives as Hewstock in Hinton St Mary Do; and a third term also meaning 'gallows' was *hēafod-trēow*, which has developed into Heavitree D. The OE word for a felon was *wearg* and the gallows where he died was a *wearg-trēow*, literally 'felon tree', as in Warter YE, or a *wearg-rōd*, literally 'felon-cross', as in Worgret Do. The valley name Tripsdale YN is derived from the OE *þrepel*, 'a wooden rack to which a body was fixed for execution' and OE *dæl*. Dethick Db was literally 'death-oak' (OE *dēað-āc*), which suggests a tree with a convenient horizontal branch from which the hangman's rope could be suspended.

It is likely that the very common place-name Friday Street (Gl, Hrt [2], K, O, Sf [6], Sx [4], Sr [2], W) was, in some instances at any rate, on the road to the gallows. In the Middle Ages, Friday was a day of ill omen, associated with the Crucifixion and with fasting. Unproductive field-plots were occasionally called 'Friday Furlong'. Many of these names now refer to farms and, in a few instances, the farm may have taken its name from the surname Friday; but there are too many of them to have all been called after this rare family name. It will be noticed, too, that 'Friday Street' is limited in distribution to the southern half of England. Fridaythorpe YE, a village name, is

127

almost certainly from the Old Scandinavian personal name *Frijádagr* or from its OE cognate, the name *Frīgedæg*.

We know very little about early Germanic heathen practices, though a few scraps of information have survived the Church's attempts to obliterate all memory of paganism. It is probable, for example, that the Lombards, at one time close neighbours of the English tribes while they were still in north Germany, made sacrifices to the head of a goat; and there are hints in the sagas that among the Scandinavian tribes the heads of animals had some significant place in their pagan worship. Tacitus records the defeat of the Roman general Varus by the Germans in AD 9. Six years later a Roman visitor to the spot saw human heads nailed to trees. He tells, too, of more northerly German tribes, including the *Anglii*, who sacrificed slaves by drowning them; and much later writers refer to human sacrifice among the heathen Saxons of the fifth and sixth centuries.

These hints scattered through the pages of ancient authors may afford a partial explanation of the many English and German place-names which refer to the heads of animals. Gateshead Du may signify a practice similar to that of the Lombards, but swinehead names are far commoner in England: Swineshead Bd, L, St; Swinehead Hundred Gl; *swines heafod* in the ancient boundaries of Calbourne Wt; Swinesherd Wo and Swinside Cu. Other words for swine are also combined with *heafod*: ON *gríss*, 'a young pig', was the first syllable of Grizehead La; OE *eofor*, 'a wild boar' has a similar position in the place-name Eversheds (Farm) in Ockley Sr. Sheep are involved in Shepshed Lei, Ramshead and Rampside La (OE *ramm*); deer in Hartshead La, YW, Hartside Cu, Nb (OE *heorot*, 'a hart'); and the badger (OE *brocc*) in Broxhead in Headley parish Ha as well as in Broxted Ess. Besides all these, there are several other animal- and bird-names with *heafod* as ending.

Perhaps even more remarkable is Manshead Hundred in Bedfordshire and the same name is on record as formerly existing in Hawton Nt and in Bottesford Lei. This name is exactly paralleled in the German place-name Mannshaúpten; and they recall a custom that is exemplified in the treatment meted out to Varus' defeated legionaries.

Tangible archaeological evidence for these barbaric practices is very limited, but highly interesting. There is a Harrow Hill at Angmering Sx which, judging from its name, was the site of a pagan Saxon religious sanctuary. It was situated within a small Iron-Age enclosure surmounting the hill. Excavations here revealed a sufficient number of ox-skulls for there to be, at an estimate, well over a thousand on the site as a whole. Probably the customary autumn slaughter of cattle took place here and the beasts' heads were offered at the shrine. A letter of Pope Gregory the Great in AD 601 to the Abbot Mellitus, a missionary to the pagan English tribes, refers to the custom of 'sacrificing many oxen (*boves*) to devils', and elsewhere, Bede records that November was called *Blōtmonath*, 'the month of blood (or sacrifice)', when the majority of the cattle were slaughtered and offerings made of them to the gods. Such a ceremony would no doubt have taken place at a local shrine (OE *hearg*, 'harrow', as in Harrow-on-the-Hill Mx), where the heads of beasts were devoted to the idols. It is just possible that different tribal groups had different animals for their sacrifices and that the animal-head names are the sole surviving evidence for most of these practices. Certainly, animal sacrifice was customary among some ancient peoples, including the Jews of the Old Testament, and its occurrence in heathen England is in no way surprising.

CHAPTER 9

Earliest English Place-Names

According to the historian Bede, who was writing in the early eighth century, three peoples came to Britain from Germany in the middle of the fifth century, the Saxons, the Angles and the Jutes. The tribal name Saxons, OE *Seaxe*, survives in the shire-names Essex (with *ēast*, 'east'), Middlesex (*middel*), and Sussex (*sūð*, 'south'), as well as in names such as Saxton C, YW, where the farms would have gained this distinctive name because they were occupied by Saxons islanded in predominantly Anglian regions. Archaeology has, in fact, revealed that women with distinctively Saxon ornaments were buried in some of the pagan cemeteries of the Cambridge region where one of the Saxtons occurs; but most of the material from the graves of this region is Anglian in type.

Saxham Sf (*hām*) and Saxondale Nt (*dæl*) also occur in regions of overwhelming Anglian predominance. On the other hand, Exton Ha, originally *æt Ēast Seaxnatūne*, 'at the farm of the East Saxons', is situated in what Bede tells us was Jutish territory. We must assume an early migration from Essex to the Meon valley to explain this name. History knows of no such event, but it was, of course, concerned with happenings on a larger scale than the trek of a few families from one part of southern England to another.

The Angles (*Engle*) did not give their name to any of the shires but, eventually, to the country as a whole, for England (*Englaland*) originally meant 'land of the Angles'. But an isolated group of them within the territory of another tribe some-

130

times retained the Anglian name. Islanded among the West Saxons in Berkshire and Devon, we find Englefield (*feld*) and Englebourne (*burna*). The Inglebys Db, L, YN (*bӯ*) are within the main region of original Anglian colonisation, but the communities they represent became isolated Anglian groups after the Danish conquest. The Ingleby villages must have been renamed or newly founded at that time. Inglewood Cu (*wudu*) was a settlement of Angles among the Britons of Cumbria.

It should be noted that the name East Anglia is a modern coinage, but its constituent counties, Norfolk and Suffolk preserve a memory of the early division of the East Angles into North Folk and South Folk. And in their continental homeland the Anglian name still survives in the district of Schleswig called Angeln. It is, in origin, the same word as OE *angel*, 'fish-hook', related to our word 'angler'. The mathematical term 'angle', which comes to us through French from the Latin *angulus*, is also related; they have a common origin, in part, with the word 'anchor'. Like East Anglia, the regional name Wessex is a modern usage.

The Jutish name does not appear to have been used of any place in Kent, in the Meon valley or the Isle of Wight; but in the remaining area where Bede tells us they had settled, namely the New Forest, there was a form of their name, *Ytene*, which did not survive beyond the early Middle Ages.

On the continent, the Saxons had the Frisians as their western neighbours. This tribe held the coastal region from the River Weser as far as modern Holland. There is archaeological evidence that some of the earliest Germanic invaders of Britain were Frisians, or had dwelt long enough among them to have acquired their styles of potting and to possess brooches of Frisian pattern. Indeed, a sixth-century writer in distant Constantinople, Procopius, asserted that our island was settled by Angles and Frisians, leaving Saxons and Jutes unmentioned. And there are at least eight place-names indicative of Frisians (*Frīsa*, *Frӯsa*, *Frēsa*) among the settlers of northern and eastern England: Freston Sf, Frieston L, Friston Sf, Fryston YW, all with *tūn*; Friezland YW (*land*), Friesthorpe L (*þorp*), Firsby L and Friesby Lei, both with *bý*. Several of these names have Scandinavian endings which could hardly have come into use before the ninth century and which may have been substitutions for original Old English words, but it has been argued that these place-names were first given during or after the Danish conquest, in which many Frisians certainly took part.

There can be little doubt, however, that a place-name such as Swaffham, C, Nf is early, for the element *hām* was already going out of use as the Anglo-Saxon conquest began to extend beyond the areas in which archaeology and history agree that the earliest settlements took place. Its meaning was 'homestead of the Swabians (*Swǣfe*)', a people who, like the Frisians, spoke a language closely resembling Old English and who, at one time, were close neighbours of the Saxons on the continent.

A less significant people were the *Spaldas*, who are represented by the modern place-names Spalding L (an *-ingas-* name, p 138), Spalding Moor and Spaldington YE. Possibly the names Spaldwick Hu (*wīc*) and Spalford Nt are other instances of settlement elsewhere by this tribe, who are mentioned in a copy of a seventh-century document, *The Tribal Hidage*, as dwellers in the fens of Huntingdonshire, Northamptonshire and Lincolnshire. The root-meaning of their name is thought to be 'ditch'; and it is just possible that each group acquired the name independently of the others from drainage channels in the Fens, perhaps those dug in Romano-British times when the region was intensely cultivated for grain. In its simple form the name is found in Holland and France. The *Spaldingas* of Spalding L may well have acquired their name from the Roman canal now called the Car Dyke, a name that did not come into use until after the Danish settlement of the region.

Less widely separated are the four place-names that commemorate another relatively minor tribe, the *Hrype*. Ribston YW (ON *steinn*, probably replacing OE *stān*, 'a stone'), Ripon YW, from the dative plural *Hrypum*, and Ripley YW (*lēah*) are not far apart, but Repton Db (*dūn*) was presumably an early off-

132

shoot of the tribe. The meaning of its name is long lost. The *Gyrwe*, on the other hand, were 'dwellers in the marsh' (OE *gyr*) and their name is enshrined in Jarrow Du, which was originally a dative plural, *Gyrwum*. Bede, who spent much of his life in the Jarrow monastery, mentions another tribe of the same name which occupied the Fenland near Peterborough Nth. This people, too, has a place in *The Tribal Hidage*.

The *Wixan*, a tribe of the Middle Saxons, finds mention in the place-names Uxbridge (*brycg*), Waxlow Farm (a *lēah* which was in Southall (*healh*) and within a mile of the ancient name Yeading (*ingas*)), and Uxendon Farm (*dūn*), which was in Harrow parish. The latter name is first recorded as *gumeninga hergae*, 'heathen temple of the people of *Guma*' (p 149). Hayes, adjacent to the parish of Southall and itself containing Yeading, was once recorded as *on linga hæse*, a primitive name of which only the final element, *hǣs*, 'brushwood', can be explained. Thus, within an area of a few miles in western Middlesex, now largely overwhelmed by the 'Great Wen', we have the tribes of the *Wixan*, *Geddingas* (Yeading), *Gumeningas* (Harrow) and, just possibly a fourth, the *Lingas*. The *Gillingas* (Ealing) were immediately to the east. It is just conceivable that this tribe had land in the waste called *Gillinga hǣs*, 'brushwood (country) of the *Gillingas*', and that the late eighth-century scribe omitted the first syllable when copying out the charter in which *linga hæse* [sic] occurs. Such omissions were not uncommon in early manuscripts when the scribe was nodding.

Modern names such as Oundle Nth and Hitchin Hrt are first recorded early and, though inexplicable with any certainty, were very probably old tribal names. The *Hicce*, whose name underlies Hitchin, were a people distinct from the *Hwicce*, who are known to have settled adjacent areas of Oxfordshire, Gloucestershire, Worcestershire and Warwickshire. Both these tribes are recorded in *The Tribal Hidage*. Wychwood O, Wichenford Wo and Whichford Wa are within the main Hwiccan territory, or near its edges, but Wichnor St (*ōfer*, 'river-bank', ie of the Trent), Whiston Nth and probably Witchley (Green) R, must represent settlement by groups or by individual families of the *Hwicce* who moved away from the main region of settlement in the south-west midlands. It is not impossible, however, that the names in Rutland and Northamptonshire came into being during the initial migration of the main Hwiccan tribe after its landing somewhere on the east coast. They would have moved westward seeking empty lands to settle. The two more easterly names would then commemorate Hwiccans who dropped out of the main band of immigrants and were left behind.

Besides these tribes who are thus remembered in place-names, there are several others mentioned in *The Tribal Hidage* and elsewhere. *Westerne, Wihtgara, Bilmiga* and *Oht gaga* are instances of peoples whose names are apparently lost altogether, though as some of the forms may well be corrupt, one cannot be sure.

It is likely that those Romano-Britons who survived the Anglo-Saxon conquest and remained in the conquered regions, either in enclaves, in family groups or as individuals, sometimes gave rise to place-names that distinguished their continuing presence from that of the neighbouring newcomers. The term *walh* in Anglian, *wealh* in West Saxon or Kentish, meant 'a foreigner, Welshman or serf'. Indeed, the modern word 'Welsh' is derived from the related adjective *Welisc*; and Wales YW, as well as the name of the principality, is from the nominative plural of the noun, namely *Walas*. A 'walnut' was OE *walhhnutu*, 'foreign nut'; and, more relevantly, the second element of Cornwall was *wealh* and the first is probably derived from a British tribal name.

Although most of the natives no doubt survived as slaves, the late seventh-century Laws of Ine, King of Wessex, speak of Welshmen holding a hide of land, enough to support a family. These men must have been free. And some such people were probably occupants of the many farms called Walton Ch, Db, Ess, K, La, Lei, Sf, Sr, St, Sx, YW, YN; but serfs of Welsh origin were probably the occupants of the hovels (*cot*) implied in Walcott or Walcot(e) Brk, L, Lei, Nf, Nth, O, Sa, W, Wa, Wo.

The inhabitants of the valleys (*denu*) called Walden Ess, Hrt, YN may have been serf or free. Other place-names with *walh* as first element are: Walbrook Lo; Walburn YN (*burna*); Wallasey Ch (originally with only OE *ēg* as termination; its Middle English derivative *ei* was added later, tautologically); Walmer K (*mere*); Walpole Sf (*pōl*) and Walworth Du, Lo (*worð*). The Wallingtons Brk, Sr were originally identical with Walton above, but Wallington Nb was 'the farm of *Walh* (the Welshman)'; Wallington Nf, 'the farm of the dwellers by the (river-) wall' (*wall*); and Wallington Hrt 'the farm of *Wændel*'s people (p 78).

Contact with the Romano-Britons resulted in the passing on of many native place-names to the new colonists. Even in the eastern parts of England, where presumably the natives survived in smaller numbers, many river-names, such as Thames, Lea, Darent, Colne and Trent are of British origin. In the west, Severn, Exe, Esk, Avon and Dee are representative of a far larger number of such survivals (p 57 f). Not a few places beside these rivers have names denoting their situation: Exeter D on the Exe, Brentford Mx on the Brent, Alnwick Nb on the Alne and Doncaster YW on the Don. And there are also town names which are wholly Celtic in origin: London, Leeds, Lyme, Eccles, Ince Ch, La and Crewe Ch, for example.

A few other words for natural features were adopted into English: *funta* (p 67) and *cumb*, 'valley', as in Whitcombe Do, Gl, W, Wt, and Widcombe So, all 'wide' (*wīd*); and, more obviously, Watercombe Do, Oxcombe L and Crowcombe So. Far less common is the word *carr*, probably a borrowing in late OE from Welsh *carn*, 'a heap of stones, a cairn', that gives us Carham Nb (dative plural, 'at the rocks'); Carhampton So, identical with the Northumbrian name until the late ninth century, when *tūn* was added, so that later there was confusion with *hāmtūn* as the ending; and Carden Ch (with *worðign*, 'enclosure'). Finally, the word *torr*, of mainly south-western distribution, as in Haytor D (*īfed*, 'overgrown with ivy') or Yar Tor (*heorot*, 'the hart'); and there are a few instances in the Peak region of Derbyshire, as for instance, Peak Tor and Row Tor. 'Row' is from OE *rūh*, 'rough'.

Hybrid names, with a Celtic first element and a Germanic ending are fairly common: Eccleshall St (*halh*, 'a corner of land'), Ecclesfield YW (*feld*, 'open country') and Eccleshill La, YW (*hyll*) have the British word *eclēsia*, 'a church' as their first element; Penhill YN, Pendle Hill La (in which '-dle' was *hyll* and a second 'hill' was added later), Pendlebury La (*hyll* plus *burh*) contain British *penno-*, 'hill'. Pendle Hill is, in effect, 'hill (British word) plus hill plus hill'. The earlier Saxons no doubt added the first 'hill' because they did not understand the meaning of 'penn' and when this compound had become Pendle by a fairly normal phonetic development, 'hill' was added again because the significance of the earlier addition had become obscured. This process of accretion was, of course, not apparent to those who used the place-name; but the hill is such a prominent one, as well as being isolated from the main Pennine ridges, that in British, early Anglian and again in later times, its name was made to emphasize and re-emphasize that it was indeed a hill.

Another important group of hybrids were Romano-British place-names with an English element, *ceaster*, 'a city', added to the older name, as for example, Winchester, Manchester, Worcester, Gloucester and Rochester. Much rarer are the instances of Celtic personal names with an Old English ending: Brixham D (possibly *Brioc* with *hām* or *hamm*; Chertsey Sr (*Cerotus* with *ēg*); Dewsbury YW (*Dewi* with *burh*); and some place-names in Chad- (*Caduc*) including Chadwick La, Wo (*wīc*), Chadstone Nth (*tūn*) and Chaddesden Db (*denu*).

It would be wrong to assume that there are necessarily numerous examples of pre-English place-names in regions where a considerable British population survived the Anglo-Saxon conquest. It is known, for instance, that the British language continued in use as late as the ninth century in Dorset, yet only about a dozen Celtic place-names are to be found there: Fontmell, possibly from *funta* (p 67) and *mēl* ('stream by a bare hill'); Pimperne, 'five trees'(?); Crichel, *crūc*, 'hill' with the explanatory addition of OE *hyll*, like Pendle (p 136); Creech (*crūc*) and several more, including some British river names. And north-western Derbyshire, a hilly region unlikely to have attracted early Anglian settlers, has a group of Celtic names strongly suggesting the persistence of British-speaking people in the area, though the number of these names is not great. Besides stream-names, such as Dove, Derwent and Clowne, there are several hill-names, including Crich and Crook Hill (*crūc*), Kinder (of obscure origin, but probably Celtic) and Mellor (*mēl* and *brigā*, 'hill'; and there are two Eccles as well as a few British woodland place-names.

Evidence for early Anglian settlement in the West Riding of Yorkshire is equally scanty. It is known from early literary works that the British kingdom of Elmet survived until it was conquered in the early sixth century by Edwin of Northumbria. Elmet is a regional name of British origin and so is Craven; Leeds, on the other hand, was in all probability a Celtic folk-name. Yet there is no great number of pre-English place-names in the Riding. Some of the names in Eccles have already been noted (p 136) and to them may be added river names such as Dearne, Dove, Wharfe, Nidd and Ure; hill-names like Penistone, Crickle and Cricklestone, and so on. In all, excluding some of doubtful etymology, there are fewer Celtic names here than might have been expected.

The name Cumberland has *Cumbre* as its first element, a borrowing into English of the Welsh *Cymry*, which was their name for themselves. In this county, and in neighbouring West-morland and Lancashire, the number of pre-English names is considerable and there can be little doubt that the region had hardly been penetrated by Anglian settlers before about AD 550, for there are none of the very earliest type of English place-names ending in -*ingas* (p 138 f) and only three in *ingaham* (p 140): Addingham, Hensingham and Whicham, all on the lower ground. The hill-country remained with the *Cumbre* until the Vikings crossed over from Ireland in the decades before and after AD 900.

137

Further to the south, in Herefordshire and Shropshire particularly, pre-English names are numerous. Indeed, moving westward from Staffordshire, Worcestershire and Gloucestershire, there is a fairly steady increase in the proportion of British names right up to the Welsh border, when English place-names cease almost completely. Roughly speaking, the proportion of pre-English place-names increases, that of English names decreases as one's eye runs across the map of western England from east to west. The earliest settlements were made in the East and South-East and it is likely that most of the British natives fled from these regions. Many of them moved towards what later became Wales; some crossed the sea to found a Little Britain, Brittany; the few who remained as slaves to the English, probably isolated from one another, had soon to acquire the rudiments of English speech. The new settlers heard so little of the British language in the eastern half of the country that they picked up few place-names from it.

It is, of course, in the East and South-East that the greatest number of very early English place-names survives. Of the earliest type, Spalding (p 132), Hastings Sx and Reading Brk are representative. Spalding is a folk-name based on a topographical feature and originally meant 'dwellers near the ditch'. Few of this type survive in use, but Sompting Sx may have been 'dwellers by the swamp' (OE *sumpt*, a word probably related to our word 'sump' and 'swamp'). The other main kind of -*ingas*-name had a personal name as first element, for example, *Hǣsta* of Hastings and *Rēada* of Reading. The meanings of these place-names were 'people of *Hǣsta* or *Rēada*' and referred originally to the inhabitants of a region and only later to the region itself. Such names finally became restricted to the main community, village or town, of these peoples.

We have already seen in the Spalding instance how such a name might recur, but with various endings, the names with a common first element sometimes being spread throughout the territory of one of these peoples. The men of Hastings, for example, occupied a large tract of land fronting the Channel between Romney Marsh on the east and the Pevensey Levels in the west. Inland, the territory probably extended to minor water-courses that delimited the land of the men of Hastings. Hasting-ford, below Hadlow Down, is over twenty-five miles from Hastings itself, at the north-western extremity of a sandstone ridge that runs almost continuously from the coast to the ford. The ridge provided an excellent main line of communication right through the territory and Hastingford was no doubt the point where the land of the *Hæstingas* was first entered from the hinterland of Sussex proper; and the smaller kingdom or prin-cipality was for long independent of the larger kingdom, for its natural boundaries were also its efficient defences from aggres-sion.

But some of these early regions, characterised by *-ingas*-names were, by contrast, quite small. An early farmstead with only a dozen or so inhabitants, representing perhaps three generations, could appropriately be referred to by an *-ingas*-name. Tyting (Farm) Sr (*Tytingas*) in St Martha's parish or Eaton (Farm) Sr (*Gēatingas*) were probably colonies consisting of only one or two family groups led by *Tyta* or *Gēat*. Sometimes different men with the same name led incoming colonists to widely separated places. The same personal name *Fēra* gave rise to Feering Ess and Ferring Sx; or perhaps these names should be derived from OE (*ge-*)*fēringas*, '(fellow) travellers'. Fringford O was a ford used by a distinct people of the same name. Barling(s) Ess, L and Birling K, Sx go back to a name such as *Bærel* or *Bærla*, whereas Patching Ess, Sx had *Pæcci* as first element. Halling K (and, formerly, Bk), Hallingbury Ess and Hallington L share the per-sonal name *Healla*; and several more such correspondences exist in the place-names of the eastern half of England.

There is a considerable number of names on the modern map which end in -ing but which have a different significance from the foregoing, though some of them may be almost as early in their formation. Within this broad category of *-ing* place-names, a number of sub-categories have been distinguished of which some include only minor places. One such group has names formed from topographical nouns, such as Bowling YW from OE *bolla*, 'a bowl' or 'a hollow'; Guiting Gl, from OE *gyte*, 'gushing', referring to a spring; and Swaythling Ha, from OE *swæð*, 'a track or swathe'. The name Wantage Brk, on the other hand, goes back to a verb, OE *wanian*, 'to wane, decrease' and referred to a stream that waned as the summer progressed. (Elsewhere, this was commonly called a 'Winterbourne'.) Adjectives, too, provided a base for some of these -*ing* names; for instance, Deeping L is from *dēop*, 'deep', the place-name meaning 'deep fen'; and Weeting Nf was a wet (OE *wēt*) place. Plant-names lie behind Clavering Ess (OE *clæfer*, 'clover') and Wratting C, Sf (*wrætt*, perhaps 'crosswort' or 'hellebore').

It is likely that most place-names ending in -ingham first came into use about a generation later than the -*ingas* names of the same region. Instances such as Birmingham and Nottingham originally consisted of a genitive plural -*inga*- with -*hām*, 'homestead' as the termination. The first syllable of such place-names is usually a personal name, *Beorma* of Birmingham, *Snot* of Nottingham, *Gylla* of Gillingham Do, K, Nf and *Billa* of Billingham Du, Sx. The name *Billa* recurs in many place-names all over the country, though it is not certainly the base of Billing Nth, which is an -*ingas* name. Billing may be derived from the personal name *Bȳdel*. There is little doubt, however, that Woking Sr and Wokingham Brk both took their names from a man called *Wocc*. It is probable that the 'people of *Wocc*' founded a daughter settlement, 'the homestead of *Wocc*'s people' at Wokingham and it is possible that Wokefield Brk was yet another and later colony of the same folk. It meant 'open country (*feld*) of *Wocc*(*a*)'. But Tillingham Ess, Sx and the two Tilburys Ess originated in the names of four distinct settlers, for no two of them are near enough together to have been named from one man.

It is worth pausing a moment to demonstrate how futile it almost always is to guess the derivation of a place-name from its modern spelling and pronunciation. The personal names in brackets in the following list are what may reasonably be postulated by a study of early forms of the place-names, the likelihood being sometimes confirmed by the occurrence of the personal name as a signature to a land charter or by an unambiguous reference to such a name in some other kind of document. Tilton Lei and Tilty Ess, the latter with *tēag*, 'a small enclosure', both have *Tila* as first element. The two Essex Tillburys (*Tilla*); Tillingham Ess and Tillingdown Sr (*Tilli*); Tillingham Sx (*Tilli* or *Tila*); Tillingbourne Sr (*Tilla*); Tillinghurst Sx (*Titta*); Tillington Sx and Tilleslow D, the latter with *slōh*, 'mire' (*Tulla*); the two Sussex Tiltons (*Tella* or *Tulla*); Tillworth D was *æt Ella*'s *worð*; Tillington He (*Tylla* or *Tylli*); Tillington St (*Titel*).

At about the same time that the place-names ending in -*inga-ham* came into use, other similar compounds were being formed, but with a different final element, as for instance -*ingaford*, -*ingadæl*, and so on. These other -*inga*- names continued to be formed until somewhat later than the -*ingahām* names. Almost always these also have a personal name as first element, sometimes of a type that went out of common use during the earlier part of the Anglo-Saxon period. Buckingham has *Bucc* and *hamm*, 'enclosure, water-meadow'; Buntingford Hrt (*Bunta, ford*); Rottingdean Sx (*Rōta, denu*); Sunningdale Brk (*Sunna, dæl*); Wellingborough Nth (*Wændel, burh*); and Wallingford (*Wealh, ford*) are instances of major place-names composed in this fashion.

There are, moreover, many names in -*ingatūn*, such as Washington Du, with the personal name *Wassa*; Litlington C (*Lȳtel(a)*) and Aldrington Sx (*Ealdhere*) that are of similar formation and antiquity as the foregoing kinds in -*inga*-, but which are difficult to distinguish from another category which also has -ington as its modern spelling. Names of this latter kind go back to OE *ingtūn* and some of them have a personal name as first element: Darlington Du (*Dēornoþ*), Workington Cu (*Weorc* or *Wyrc*), Bridlington YE (*Berhtel*), Erdington Wa (*Earda*), Bebbington Ch (*Bebba*) and Kensington Lo (*Cynesige*) are some of the better-known examples of this type. The meaning was

'*Dēornop*'s farm' and so on, almost the equivalent of a genitive singular plus *tūn*; whereas an -*ingatūn* name such as Aldrington Sx was 'the farm of the *Ealdheringas*', that is, 'of *Ealdhere*'s people'.

Besides this type with a personal name plus -*ingtūn*, there occurred another in which the -*ing*- originated in various other Old English words or syllables. For instance, Abingdon Brk was *Æbbandun* in its original form, meaning '*Æbba*'s hill'; the frequently recurring Newington had 'new' (*nīwe, nīowe*) in the dative singular, '(*æt*) *þǣm nīwan tūne*', '(at) the new farm' (p 78); Withington Ch, He, La, Sa had *wīðign*, 'willow' or *wiðigen*, 'growing with willows' as the first element; and Haslingden La was 'the valley (*denu*) growing with hasels (*hæslen*)'; and see p 51. As may be seen from these examples, the medial syllable -ing- is a misunderstanding and had various origins. The change was made easier because there were so many place-names with an original -*ing*-; the false ones were made unconsciously by analogy with the true ones.

Finally -*ing*- was sometimes used as a connective linking river-names with other elements, as in Leamington Wa (River Leam) and Cockerington L (River Cocker).

Another method of detecting very early place-names is by the vocabulary used in them. A number of the -*ingas* and -*inga*-types are based on personal names that do not occur in the relatively few surviving Old English documents, but which have cognates in earlier or contemporary use among the Germanic peoples of the Continent. For instance, Dullingham C is explained as 'the homestead of *Dull(a)*'s people' and, although *Dulla* is not one of the many names known to have been borne by Angles or Saxons, there is a recorded Old High German *Dolleo* which is a true cognate. Similarly, Minting L seems to be based on an unrecorded personal name *Mynta*, paralleled by the known OHG *Munizo*.

Of a somewhat different kind is the place-name Naseby Nth, which before the Danish conquest had been called *Hnæfes burh*, 'fortress of *Hnæf*'. This was not a name in ordinary use among

the Anglo-Saxons, but one apparently reserved to the hero
Hnæf, the Half-Dane, Lord of the *Hocingas,* who is referred to in
the poems *Bēowulf, Wīdsīð* and elsewhere. This name is not recorded outside heroic poetry. Nevendon Ess, '(*H*)*nefa*'s valley
(*denu*)' has a lost OE personal name related to *Hnæf,* but only
known otherwise from its OHG cognate *Nefi.* In the same
county, Elsenham has either *Elesa* or *Elsa* as first element. In
the royal genealogy of Wessex, a document of very ancient origin, Cerdic, the leader of the English invasion of central
southern Britain in *c* AD 495, is said to have been the '*son of
Elesa* (who was) son of *Esla*'. These two tribal leaders belong
then to the early and middle fifth century.

Massingham Nf and Messingham L, originally identical in
form, and Marsworth Bk, had OE *Mæssa,* a personal name unrecorded in Old English but again paralleled in OHG in the form
Mas(*s*)*o.* In Middlesex, the places Wembley and Fulham contain the names *Wemba* and *Fulla* respectively, both otherwise
unknown in England, though there was a Gothic king *Wamba.*
And several other personal names could be cited which had
become obsolete within a generation or so of the Anglo-Saxon
conquest and which may be assumed only as a result of the
study of place-names.

Personal nomenclature, like pronunciation, spelling, syntax
and grammar had been evolving before the fifth century and
continued to do so afterwards, though the causes of change were
themselves changing from time to time. After the fifth century,
slighter contacts with the other Germanic peoples and with the
diluted Latin cultures of the old Roman provinces, had some
effect; and the new proximity to the Celtic cultures of Britain
was a positive factor in the development of personal nomenclature. Within the conquered regions of Britain, divergent
changes in language were produced by the relative isolation of
Anglo-Saxon kingdoms and sub-kingdoms one from another.
Moreover, the conversion to Christianity, beginning in the early
seventh century, opened up a broad channel along which the
late Roman culture of Italy herself could flow and the language

143

underwent a strong infusion of words borrowed from Latin to express ideas that could only be clumsily encompassed from the Old English vocabulary. As we have seen, the Danish and Norman conquests had their great influence, too.

There were a number of words in the vocabulary of the earlier Anglo-Saxon settlers that soon fell out of use. The most important and commonest was *hām*, which occurs in most Germanic languages: Gothic *haims*, Old Saxon *hem*, Old High German *heim* and Old Norse *heimr*, denoting 'a village' or 'dwelling-place', both of which meanings are evident in OE texts. Later in Old English it could mean 'a manor, an estate, a household, a monastery', but the most usual sense was 'village', especially after the initial period of settlement.

This element is far less common in the North-West, the Midlands and South-West, regions which were settled later than the rest of England. It occurs frequently in regions where *-ingas* place-names and archaeology attest early colonisation and for this reason alone should be regarded as an important part of the early Old English place-name vocabulary. The fact that it is sometimes compounded with *inga-* (p 141) and early types of personal names (p 142 f) tends to confirm that conclusion. Examples of *-hām* names have already been given in considerable numbers, including the early type-*ingahām* (p 140); and, as has already been remarked, the element *-hām* is a quite common feature of early place-names. But there are still a few others worthy of mention though they are of rarer occurrence.

Tyburn Lo, the old place of execution near the modern Marble Arch, was originally the name of a brook (*burna*). The first element occurs in an OE charter as *tēo*, a word cognate with and meaning the same as Frisian *tia*, 'a boundary-(line)'. Another charter calls the same brook *merfleot*, a compound of (*ge-*)*māre*, 'boundary' and *flēot*, 'stream', which is synonymous with *tēo-burna*. No doubt the second name came into use as the first ceased to be intelligible, for *tēo* had ceased to be a part of the later vocabulary. Teffont W has this same word, but combined with *funta* (p 67), the whole meaning 'boundary spring or stream'. It presumably marked the ancient division between the lands of the people of Dinton ('*Dunna*'s farm') and those of Chilmark (*cegel*, 'pole' used as a boundary-mark [*mearc*]).

It is noteworthy, too, that *burna* was being used in place-name formation only during the settlement period and that at an early date it was supplanted by *brōc*, 'brook, stream'. The term *burna* is found in combination with *hām* in several Burnhams (p 60), but it does not occur with *tūn*, an element that continued to be used in forming place-names for long after *hām* had become obsolete. The words *hām* and *tūn* were partly synonymous and *tūn* came to be used where formerly *hām* would have conveyed the appropriate sense. In the North, however, the introduction of the ON *brunnr* gave rise to the modern word 'burn' in the sense 'brook' and this usage probably spread southwards, eventually in the form 'bourn' and came to be used widely as a generic word for stream. It is to be distinguished from another word 'bourn' which is derived from Old French *borne*, 'boundary', limit', as in Hamlet's:

> . . . *death,*
> *The undiscovered country from whose bourn*
> *No traveller returns.*

The noun 'bound', in the sense 'limit, boundary' (as in 'to beat the bounds') is also of French origin, namely OF *bonde*.

The word *gē*, 'district, region', fell into disuse even before *tēo* and its significance has had to be deduced in part from its cognates in other Germanic languages. In England it occurred in the second syllable of Ely C, 'the eel (*ēl*) district'. Bede called Ely a region: *in regione quae vocatur Elge*; and eels as rent in kind were a valuable form of income for the great monastery of Ely. The shire-name Surrey has this element, too; it is combined with *sūðer*, 'south, southern' and it suggests that this ancient province had a northern counterpart, which could only have been that of the Middle Saxons who occupied roughly what we now call Middlesex. In the names Suffolk and Norfolk (p 131) we may well have an analogy: of a larger unit, the East Anglian kingdom in this instance, divided into two by the rivers Waveney and Little Ouse in the same way as the Thames divided the men of Surrey from the Middle Saxons.

Eastry K, 'the easterly (*ēastor*) region', was central to the eastern part of Kent in early Jutish times. Sturry K and Lyminge K were regions characterised by the rivers Stour and Lympne; Denge K, 'valley (*denu*) region', seems to have had its marshland grazing grounds on Denge (Dunge) Marsh, behind Dungeness. Adjacent to Denge Marsh was (the) Burmarsh, over which the rights of grazing were held by the *Burhware*, the men of Canterbury, known in the eighth century as *Cantwaraburg*, literally, 'Kent-dwellers' city'. Vange Ess, the only other certain instance of the use of *gē* in place-names, was the 'fen (*fenn*) district'.

The first syllable of Earith Hu and Erith K was the ancient word *ēar*, 'gravel, mud, earth'; the second was *hȳð*, 'landing-place'. Yarmouth Wt has the same first syllable and *mūða*, 'estuary'. (But Yarmouth Nf meant 'mouth of the River Yare', a Celtic river-name.)

And there are three words occurring in Sussex place-names that are probably of equal antiquity. The term *glind* has already been noted (p 82) as one of the many words for 'enclosure'. Just as rare in surviving place-names, though more widespread, is *etisc(e)*, '(pasture-) land', which is found in the name Cleeve Axe Sx, with *clif*, 'steep slope' and in such medieval Sussex field-names as *Brodenexe*, with OE *brād*, 'broad' or Ferthex, with OE *fyrhðe*, 'woodland'. Duntish Do has *dūn*, 'hill' and Wrantage So has *wrǣna*, 'a stallion'. In Broomhill Sx we have another term that was obsolete early, namely OE *prūme*, a plum', which had been borrowed from the Latin *prunus* before the migrations to Britain.

It is no coincidence that these words, obsolete before the lapse of a few generations after the Anglo-Saxon conquest, are from those regions that had been among the first to be seized. The new lands further west were colonised by new immigrants from overseas or by the younger men and women sprung from the earliest settlers. For these offspring there was too little good land or none in the regions of primary settlement. In naming the features of their new lands, they unconsciously used a vocabulary different in minor respects from that of their immediate forebears, and in doing so they unwittingly provided us with evidence for changes in vocabulary. And, though it is beyond the scope of this book to offer details, they demonstrated also minor developments in syntax, pronunciation and personal nomenclature.

The final category of early place-names consists of those which designated the places of heathen worship. In AD 597 *Æðelbryht*, king of Kent, was converted to Christianity and in 604 the East Saxon king also accepted it. Edwin of Northumbria followed in about 627 and a few years later there were missions to the East Angles. The king of Wessex, Cynegils, was baptised in 635, but it was nearly twenty years before a beginning was made with the conversion of the Middle Angles and not until 680 that the South Saxons began to receive the faith. But the general abandonment of heathen beliefs did not occur merely because a king was baptised. As early as 616, *Eadbald* of Kent apostasised and returned to pagan custom, only to be converted again later. As much as five years after the conversion of Eadwine of Northumbria, we learn of the destruction of a heathen temple at Goodmanham YE by a chief priest who had just seen the new light. The baptism of the king of Wessex in 635 did not affect his son, who for long held to the old beliefs. There was a partial relapse from Christianity in Northumbria and the real conversion of the East Saxons did not begin until half a century after one of their kings had been baptised. The re-establishment of Christianity in Northumbria occurred hardly before 670. In short, heathen beliefs had a very tenacious hold on the minds of the English and even long after the conversion of a court, there might be many, even of those within its ambit, who continued to cling to the old faith. *Eorconberht* of Kent (640–64), son of the apostate *Eadbald*, had to forbid heathen practices and order the destruction of idols; and, even later, *Wihtred* (690–725) enacted a law against the custom of sacrificing to devils.

147

Nevertheless, it is very doubtful whether heathen temples were established anywhere, or a name given to them, after about AD 700 and place-names implying a belief in the pagan gods almost all belong to the first two centuries of the English settlement in Britain.

The war-god *Tīw* or *Tīg* is commemorated in Tewin Hrt, an *-ingas*-name; in Tysoe Wa (*hōh*, 'a hill-spur'); in Twiscombe D (*cumb*, 'a valley'); Tuesley Sr (*lēah*, 'a wood'); and Tuesnoad K (*snād*, 'a detached piece of land or of a wood'), as well as in the word 'Tuesday'. The god *þunor*, whose name survives in 'Thursday', was the god of thunder, a word directly derived from his name. He was probably less venerated by the Anglian tribes, for place-names relating to him are not found in their territories. Among the Saxons he was worshipped at Thunderley and Thundersley Ess (both with *lēah*), at Thunderfield Sr (*feld*, 'open country') and at Thursley Sr (*lēah*), as well as at Thundridge Hrt (*hrycg*) and at places in Sussex, Hampshire and Wiltshire of which the names have not survived into modern use, but are known only from early documents.

Wōden (or its variant *Wēden* of 'Wednesday'), who was god of the dead and of mighty earthworks—too great, apparently, to have been heaped up by ordinary men—was associated with the Wansdyke Ha, So, W (*dīc*) and some minor sites topographically related to it; with barrows such as Wenslow Bd (*hlāw*) or, possibly Woodnesborough K, of which the second element was *beorg*. This could mean either 'hill' or 'barrow', but the latter sense may well have been the one intended, for the Jutes of Kent were accustomed to inter their dead under barrows and there were formerly many groups of small ones in eastern Kent. An exact parallel to the name Woodnesborough exists in the long-lost name *Wodnes beorh*, which is close to the Wansdyke in Wiltshire. The barrow itself, however, still remains, very stark on the skyline. It dates, in fact, from the early Neolithic period and its apparent size is cunningly enhanced by its placing; its size was probably the reason for its nominal association with *Woden*. It was renamed Adam's Grave and is so recorded on the modern map, the renaming being no doubt a result of pressure from early churchmen who sought to eradicate all heathen associations. There were large barrows, too, in East Kent. At Breach Down one of the Jutish tumuli was 132 ft in circumference and 8 ft high in the mid-nineteenth century after more than a thousand years of erosion. It may reasonably be said then that there is no improbability in suggesting that Woodnesborough may have meant 'Woden's barrow', for the barrow itself could have been destroyed long ago like so many others in Kent. If, however, we took *beorg* in this name to 'mean 'hill', there is a parallel to that also. It exists in the place-name Wormshill K which appears is a thirteenth-century document in the spelling *Wodnesell*. It should be noted that the final *-ell* represents OE *hyll* with the loss of 'h' and a change of *y* to *e*, which was already appearing in Kentish documents of the tenth century.

The place-names Wednesbury (*burh*) and Wednesfield (*feld*) St, Wensley Db (*lēah*) and Wenslow Bd, already mentioned, are from the mutated form, *Wēden*, of the god's name.

But not all pagan sites bore the name of gods; many of the place-names associated with them refer merely to a temple or shrine. Harrow-on-the-Hill Mx, for example, was called (*æt*) *gumeninga hergæ* [sic], 'at the heathen temple of the *Gumeningas*' (p 133) in the eighth century. Harrowden Bd, Ess, Nth, all with *dūn*, are similarly hill sites and Arrowfield (Top) Wo seems to suggest a similar situation. Peper Harow Sr is interesting for a different reason, in that the first element was the name, *Pipera*, of the owner of the temple. There is a parallel to this in the ancient lost place-name *Cusan weoh*, '*Cusa*'s shrine', which was somewhere in west Surrey. Patchway Sx was '*Pæccel*'s shrine' (*wēoh*). This term *wēoh* occurs also in hill-names: Waden W, Weedon Bk, Nth (all three with *dūn*); with *ford* in Weeford St; and notably as a woodland-name in Weeley Ess, Weoley Wo and Wheely (Farm) Ha (all with *lēah*). The related word *wīg*, which also meant 'idol' or 'shrine', is also found combined with *lēah*, 'wood', as in the minor Sussex places Whiligh and Whyly and in Willey Sr. Wyfold O, Bk meant 'idol or shrine enclosure' (*fald*); Wyham L is a dative plural with some such meaning as 'at the shrines' and Wyeville L has *wella* as its second element, probably here meaning 'a spring'. Wye K was simply *wēoh* and Weyhill Ha was originally identical with Wye, the word 'hill' being an addition after the fifteenth century.

In Alkham K (*hām*) we have the term *ealh*, 'heathen temple', which otherwise is found only in a long disused minor place-name elsewhere in Kent and in Old English poetry.

It is noteworthy how many of these pagan temples were placed on hills. It is likely that every community, or adjacent groups of settlements, had each a heathen sanctuary, but that the names and hence the locations, of very few have survived. It was suggested long ago that Harrow church Mx, on its hill-top, was successor to the temple that gave the place its name. Very many old parish churches are situated on ground higher than the original centres of the villages and it is possible that some, at any rate, of these churches are successors on the same site to pagan shrines, for continuity of worship was strongly enjoined by Pope Gregory in a letter to the Abbot Mellitus as he was about to set out on a mission to the English in AD 601: 'The temples of the idols . . . must not be destroyed, but the temples themselves should be sprinkled with holy water, altars set up and (Christian) relics enclosed in them. As a result, we hope that the people . . . will give up heathen beliefs and go to their temples as they had been accustomed to do . . . (Bede, *Ecclesiastical History*, 1, 30). The Roman historian Tacitus, writing in AD 97–98, apparently of the *Suebi* (OE *Swǣfe*, p 132), but probably of the West Germanic tribes in general, observed their that religious sanctuaries were the woods and groves and that they gave the name 'god' to the hidden presence which only the devout may see (Germania §9). The pagan place-names in -*lēah* seem to confirm this statement.

There is another group of place-names that may have first come into use before the coming of Christianity to southern Britain. Each has as first element God- or Gad- in the modern form of the name; and since a personal name *God* is recorded in

150

the Wiltshire section of the Domesday Book, the place-names of this group are usually derived in part from this personal name. However, proper nouns of all kinds are sometimes unrecognisable in the Domesday Book; they vary greatly from spellings of forms both before and after 1086. For example, *Nigavre* for Netheravon W contrasts strongly with twelfth-century forms like *Ned(h)eravena, Netheravena*. No forms earlier than 1086 have survived. The scribes of the Domesday survey had a scanty knowledge, if any, of Anglo-Saxon speech and they were of necessity recording the statements of peasant jurors whose enunciation may well have been poor. The old and toothless would have been the villagers called on to dig back into memories of a generation earlier. The scribes did their best to render proper names, using their own conventions of orthography to represent sounds in a strange language and with a strange intonation and accentuation. Some of the Old English sounds did not exist in Norman-French. It is scarcely surprising that the scribes sometimes failed dismally in their recording.

But a further objection to the occurrence of a personal name common to this group of place-names is that there survive six instances of the compound 'god' with 'hill': Godshill Ha, Sx, Wt, Godsell (Farm) W and Gadshill, twice found in Kent. Coincidence is strained too far if we assume that this alleged personal name was applied mainly to hills: analogies for this are unknown, even of a very common personal name and this is a rare one. Indeed, in most counties, few personal names occur at all in combination with *hyll* and the few that do came into use long after the coming of Christianity. Altogether, then, the evidence is strongly against the first element of Godshill and Gadshill being a personal name. The few other probable instances of this first element are: Godsfield Ha (*feld*), Godswell (Grove) W (*wella*) and Gadsey (Brook) Bd (*ēg*). In Godstow O we have the Christian deity as part of the name of a nunnery consecrated in 1138. The name did not exist earlier. It meant 'place dedicated to God'.

It is possible that Godley (Bridge) Sr, Ch and Godney So have

151

the same word *god* in the genitive plural, *godena*, and that they meant 'grove of the gods' and 'island of the gods'. Certainly, *god* was used of the heathen gods or of an idol and it is likely that the early form of Wormshill K (p 149), namely *Godeshelle*, was an alternative, 'the god's hill', for the more usual name 'Woden's hill'. Possibly this was a deliberate ambiguity between 'god' and 'God' or, more likely, it may represent an unsuccessful attempt to rename the hill in the same fashion that *Wodnes beorg* became Adam's Grave (pp 148–9).

In its counterblasts against heathenism it is certain that the Church had only a small success and that many pagan names and practices survived, usually in barely recognisable forms though even into the twentieth century. The practices and the beliefs that underlay them, which are probably implied by some of the names ending in -head (pp 128–9), may have faded early; and possibly few people were conscious that the names of the ancient gods were upon their lips when they uttered such place-names as Thursley and Wednesbury or referred to the days of the week.

But there were lesser beings from the supernatural world who continued for at least a thousand years after the Conversion to play a shadowy part in the minor dramas of ordinary people's lives. Shakespeare's Puck had an antecedent, *pūca*, 'a goblin', in Anglo-Saxon times. His general attributes may have been different, but his ubiquity in some regions, Sussex for instance, is attested by the association of his name with many fields and several minor topographical features of the countryside. Essex, Hampshire, Gloucestershire and Wiltshire had similar local hauntings. Puckeridge Hrt, with either *hrycg*, 'ridge' or *ric*, 'stream', and Purbrook Ha (*brōc*) are two of the larger places associated with goblins. The diminutive, *pūcel(a)* occurs in such names as Puxton Wo and Pucklechurch Gl, perhaps in the form of a by-name of the owners, rather than in the literal sense 'little goblin'.

Other beings, generally more malevolent, were commemorated in place-names such as Shacklow Db, Shugborough St and Shuckburgh Wa. In these *scucca*, 'a demon' or 'an evil spirit' was associated with a barrow (*hlāw*), an old earthwork (*burh*) and a hill or barrow (*beorg*). But it is the dragon (*draca*) that was most commonly linked with barrows in the popular mind. Drakelow Bd, Db, Wo calls to mind the last fatal fight of Beowulf against the fire-breathing dragon, guardian of a precious hoard beneath a barrow. It also calls to mind the magnificent treasure found in a barrow, a princely cenotaph, at Sutton Hoo, Suffolk; the Taplow treasure from another great barrow; and of other lesser barrow finds of the Saxon period. Drake North Ha, a minor place in the parish of Damerham, was *drakenhorde* in the tenth century and no doubt a hoard of treasure was once found there, such a treasure that a dragon must once have stood guard over it. Perhaps these stories of vigilant monsters were first put around to deter treasure-seekers who were violators of graves, but apparently the stories gained credence and became widespread. A barrow-hoard was at least thought to exist at Hurdlow Db and treasures of various kinds were presumably found at Hordle Ha (*hyll*), and Hordley Sa (*lēah*). Springs or wells (*wella*) at Hardwell Brk and Orwell (Bury) Hrt were no doubt places into which valuables were cast for luck.

But there were other places besides barrows that were haunted by dragons. A valley (*dæl*) was thus terrorised at Drakedale YN and Drakehill Sr is a high natural mound, topped by the medieval chapel of St Catherine, situated just south of Guildford. This is an instance of a place beset with heathen superstition that was hallowed for Christian purposes. In addition to these instances of dragon-names there are a few others up and down the country.

Dwarfs (*dwerg*) were not necessarily imaginary beings and may have been more numerous in early times than today. They do not figure often in place-names, but Dwariden YW was a valley (*denu*) that was frequented by them at one time and presumably Dwerryhouse La (*hūs*) had its name from diminutive people who built dwellings there. Very occasionally, old field-names refer to them. We know, however, that giants (*ent*) were imagined to have had a hand in buildings that seemed to the early English beyond the scope of ordinary men, for the Anglo-

153

Saxons built with timber and the Britain they conquered had ruins of stone and brick structures of which the origin and construction were mysterious. In the Old English poem 'The Wanderer' there is mention of the 'old work of giants' (*eald enta geweorc*) that stood empty and, by implication of the context, were ruined—possibly a reference to western and south-western hill-forts with ramparts built of great blocks of stone. The Gnomic verses of a somewhat earlier period have a fuller allusion in:

> . . . *Ceastra bēoð feorran gesȳne,*
> *orðanc enta geweorc, þā þe on þysse eorðan syndon,*
> *wrǣtlic weallstana geweorc;*

which may be translated: 'Cities (chesters) are seen from afar, the cunning work of giants, which are on this earth, wondrous work of wallstones.' London, Winchester, Leicester, Verulamium, Chester, York and other Roman cities, as they appeared in the fifth century, before the English began to occupy the more habitable ruins, may have been in the poet's mind's eye when he wrote this. The term *ceaster* (p 136) was most commonly applied to Roman cities, less often to their forts or country houses, all of which are likely to have been ruinous by early Saxon times. Even in the poem 'The Ruin', where the poet more obviously has a Roman city in mind and imagines its former human inhabitants, giants are said to have been the builders.

Nevertheless, the word *ent* survives in only one minor place-name, Indescombe (Tavistock) D and as it is used in the genitive singular, one cannot be sure that it was not a by-name for a very tall dweller in the valley. But, another word, *þurs*, with the same meaning, is commoner. It is the first syllable of Thrushgill La (*gil*, 'a ravine'); and in its mutated form *þyrs*, it occurs in Thirlspott Cu, with Middle English *potte*, 'a deep hole (in a river-bed)', in Thursden La (*denu*), Trusey YE (*haugr*, 'hill') and Tusmore O (*mere*). The first element of Tusmore, however, may have been the name of the heathen god, *þunor*, for this was a region of early settlement where a pagan place-name could well occur. There was a pagan Saxon cemetery at Souldern, only about two miles from Tusmore, which yielded Anglo-Saxon pottery made before AD 500.

BOOKS MOST OFTEN CONSULTED

Volumes I–XLIII of The English Place-Name Society.

E. Ekwall, *English River-Names* (1928).

E. Ekwall, *Street-Names of the City of London* (1954).

E. Ekwall, *Oxford Dictionary of English Place-Names*, 2nd Edn (1940).

W. Little and others, *Shorter Oxford English Dictionary*, 3rd Edn, (1947), revised by C. T. Onions.

C. T. Onions, *Oxford Dictionary of English Etymology* (1966).

J. Bartholomew, *Survey Gazetteer of the British Isles*, 9th Edn (1943).

G. J. Copley, *Names and Places* (1963).

Elements in Place-Names

157

162

Index of Place-Names

164

Durham, 66
Durfold Co, Sr, 81
Durley Ha, 22
Dwariden YW, 153
Dwerryhouse La, 153

Ealing Mx, 133
Eamont Cu, 62
Earith Hu, 146
Earl's Barton Nth, 11, 78
Earl's Croome Wo, 12
Earlshaw Nt, 11
East Bridgford Nt, 64
Easter Ess, 81
Eastfield freq, 107
Eastleach Gl, 32, 62
Eastoft L, YW, 44
Eastover So, 108
Eastry K, 146
Eaton freq, 61
Eaton (Fm) Sr, 139
Eau C, L, 61
Eccles Db, La, Nf, 135, 137
Ecclesfield YW, 136
Eccleshall St, 136
Eccleshill La, YW, 136
Edge Ch, Gl, Sa, 94
Edgbaston Street Wa, 108
Edgfield Nf, 82
Edgeley Ch, Sa, 82
Edgeworth La, Gl, 94
Eelmere YE, 117
Eldmire YN, 28
Elham K, 30
Ellerbeck Cu, La, YW, 43
Ellershaw Cu, 117
Ellerton, YN, YW, 43
Elmet YW, 137
Elmham Nf, 42
Elmley K, Wo, 42, 48
Elmstead Ess, K, 42
Elsage Bk, 80
Elsenham Ess, 143
Elste(a)d Sf, Sr, 44
Elstob Du, 44
Elterwater La, 29
Elvetham Ha, 28
Ely C, 30, 145
Emmetts La, 62
Enborne Brk, 28
Endcliff Db, 28
Enfield Mx, 86

Englebourne D, 131
Englefield Brk, 131
Entwisle La, 62
Erdington Wa, 141
Eridge Sx, 27
Erith K, 146
Escombe Du, 82
Escrick YE, 44
Esk, river, Cu, YN, 57, 135
Essex, 130
Etchells Ch, Db, 93
Eton Bk, 61
Everley W, YN, 34
Eversheds Sr, 128
Eversley Ha, 34
Everton Bd, La, Nt, 34
Ewell K, Sr, 68
Ewelme O, 68
Ewen Gl, 68
Ewhurst Ha, Sr, Sx, 49
Exbourne D, 25
Exe, river, So, D, 57, 135
Exeter D, 58, 135
Exmouth D, 58
Exton Ha, 130
Eyam Db, 65
Eye Brook La, 61

Fairley Sa, 54
Fairlight Sx, 54
Faldingworth La, 118
Falkland So, 45
Fareham Ha, 54
Farleigh freq, 54
Farnborough Brk, K, 54
Farndale YN, 54
Farndish Bd, 82
Farndon Ch, Nt, 54
Farne Islands Nb, 67
Far(n)ley St, YW, 54
Farnham Bk, K, Sr, YW, 54
Farnworth La, 78
Far(r)ington Brk, Do, 54
Farsley YW, 53
Faulkland So, 45
Faxton Nth, 41
Felton freq, 50
Fenby L, 74
Fenkle Street freq, 111
Fenton freq, 74
Fenwick Nb, YW, 74
Fernworthy D, 79

173

Peper Harow Sr, 149
Pepper Lane Wa, 106
Pepper Street Nt, 106
Perry Hu, K, St, 51
Perton St, 51
Pesthouse Lane Mx, 103
Pett K, 95
Pevensey Sx, 48
Pickburn YW, 117
Pickhill Ess, 116
Pick Hill K, 116
Pickmere Ch, 117
Pickthorn Sa, 117
Pickup Bank La, 116
Pickworth L, Ru, 117
Picton Ch, YN, 117
Piece freq, 88
Piend D, 80
Pigdon Nb, 116
Pike o' Stickle We, 116
Pilton So, 69
Pin (Grn) Hrt, 80
Pinfold Nb, 80, 101
Pinkhurst Sr, Sx, 25
Pinnock(s) Ha, Gl, W, 80
Pirbright Sr, 49
Pirton Hrt, Wo, 51
Pitt Ha, 95
Pla(i)sh Sa, So, 70
Plashet(t) Ess, Sr, Sx, 82
Plashford Co, 70
Plasset Nf, 82
Platt(s) freq, 88
Pleck(s) freq, 88
Pleshey Ess, 82, 96
Plessey Nb, 82
Plumley Ch, 51
Plumpton freq, 51
Pollard YE, 69
Plot(s) Nt, YW, 88
Pool(e) Ch, D, Do, Gl, YW, 69
Poorhouse Hill Sx, 103
Porlock So, 81
Portbury So, 28
Portgate Nb, 28
Portland Do, 28
Portmill Lane Hrt, 108
Portway freq, 111
Poulders K, 69
Poulton freq, 69
Poultry Cross, 100
Pound (Fm) freq, 80, 101

Poundfield Sx, 80
Poundisford Co, 80
Poundstock Co, 80
Powderham D, 69
Puckeridge Hrt, 152
Pucklechurch Gl, 152
Puddle Dock Lo, Ess, Sx, 70
Punda YE, 80
Purbrook Ha, 152
Purton Gl, St, W, 51
Pusey Brk, 38,
Putley He, 27
Putney Lo, 27, 73
Puttenham Sr, 27
Puxton Wo, 152
Pyrton O, 51, 77

Quantock So, 58
Quarles Nf, 95
Quarndon Db, 97
Quarrendon Bk, 97
Quarrington Du, 97
Quay Street freq, 73, 108
Queen Camel So, 58
Quinton Gl, Nth, Wo, 9
Quorn(don) Lei, 97

Radbourn(e) Db, Wa, 39
Radipole Do, 39
Radwinter Ess, 83
Rae Burn Cu, 22
Raise Cu, 123
Raisthwaite La, 123
Rampton C, Nt, 20
Ramsbottom La, 20
Ramsey Ess, Hu, 52
Ramsgate K, 85
Ramshead La, 128
Rampside La, 128
Ravenscar YN, 98
Ravenscroft Ch, 26
Ravensden Bd, 26
Ravensthorpe Nth, YN, 26
Rawreth Ess, 27
Ray, river, O, Bk, 61
Rayhead YW, 23
Rayton Nt, 13
Rea, river, C, Sa, Wa, Wo, 61
Reading Brk, 91, 138
Reading Ess, K, 91
Reaveley Nb, 13
Redbourn Hrt, L, 39

179

180

184

General Index

187

GENERAL INDEX

pre-English names, 57 f, 69, 135 f
pronunciation, 8, 51, 53
Puck, 152
pyres, *see* cremation

rabbits, 23
raids, Danish, French, 11–12, 36, 66, 96–7, 112
relapses into paganism, 147
reversion of arable to waste, 39, 55–6
river-names, 57–63, 135, 137
Roman buildings, 18, 28, 43, 48, 67, 77, 81, 132, 133 f, 154
Romano-Britons, 37, 49, 56, 67, 75, 118, 131 f
Roman roads, 99, 110–11

salt, 43, 63, 104, 105, 111
Saxons, 130, 145, 147, 148
Scandinavians, 115, 128
scars (rocky outcrops), 97–8
scrubland, 55 f
sea, 69, 74
sea inlets, 71 f
secondary settlement, 36, 72, 90 f, 146–7
social classes, 7, 8, 11, 12, 16, 20
soils, 50, 72, 76
spelling, 8, 19
springs and wells, 9, 63, 67 f, 94–5, 102, 117, 119, 153
Stow, John, 102, 109
street-names, 99 f
studs of horses, 18, 81
substitution of a word for an obsolete one, 13–14, 41, 62
substitution of Scandinavian words for English ones, 34, 45, 60, 81, 142–3
suburbs, names of streets, 112–13

superstitions, 9, 73, 152 f
surnames, 8, 31, 61, 109, 127
survival of Britons or their language, 64, 134, 136 f
Sutton Hoo burial, 34, 54, 153
Swabians, 132, 150
swine pastures, 17, 29, 121

Tacitus, 128, 150
tautology, 28, 49, 69, 71, 80, 89, 90, 124, 126, 135, 136, 137
temples, pagan, 129, 147 f
tenure of land, 45, 81
Til- place names, 140–1
trade, 56, 64
transhumance, 115
treasure hoards, 153
trees, 41 f, 59
Tribal Hidage, 132 f
tribal names, 130 f
tūn, meanings, 77–8, 124–5

valley names, 83, 87, 89, 117
Vikings, 10–12, 36, 66, 112
village defences, 33, 95–6
vineyards, 83
vocabulary of Anglo-Saxons, 8, 68, 142 f, 147

warriors, 10, 40
water supplies, 67–8, 102, 119, *and see* springs
wells, *see* springs
West Saxons, 131, 143, 147, 148
wīc names, 30, 40
wild animals, 22 f
woodland occupations, 13
worth(y) names, 78–9, 118–19
writing, 45

188